The Risorgimento: Thought and Action

The Risorgimento:

Translated by
Mario Domandi

Introduction by
Charles F. Delzell

Thought and Action

LUIGI SALVATORELLI

HARPER TORCHBOOKS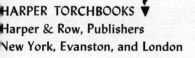
Harper & Row, Publishers
New York, Evanston, and London

Translation © 1970 by Mario Domandi.

THE RISORGIMENTO: THOUGHT AND ACTION

Copyright © 1970 by Luigi Salvatorelli.

Introduction © 1970 by Charles F. Delzell.

All rights reserved. Printed in the United States of America. No
part of this book may be used or reproduced in any manner whatsoever
without written permission except in the case of brief quotations
embodied in critical articles and reviews. For information
address Harper & Row, Publishers, Inc., 49 East 33rd Street,
New York, N.Y. 10016.

First HARPER TORCHBOOK edition published 1970

LIBRARY OF CONGRESS CARD CATALOG NUMBER: 73-145683

Contents

IV. THE DEFINITE FORMULATION

V. THE NATIONAL REVOLUTION

Introduction

In the spring of 1943, when Mussolini's Black Shirt regime was mired down in a war that almost every Italian knew by then was lost, a small book bearing the title *Pensiero e azione del Risorgimento* was published in Turin by the house of Einaudi. The author of this book on the thought and action of the Italian unification era was Luigi Salvatorelli, a prolific journalist and democratic-liberal historian whose unconcealed contempt for Fascism had kept him largely in eclipse for many years. The appearance of Salvatorelli's interpretive essay at that time offered conclusive evidence to many of his readers that the dictatorship must be on its last legs, for the passionate contents were a challenge to and a repudiation of most of the ultranationalistic and reactionary theses that had been set forth about the Risorgimento by the Fascist-approved "court historians." Certainly the study could not easily have slipped by the censors a few years before. What was in some cases still implicit in the 1943 edition was made explicit in the postwar editions that included a final chapter, "The Post-Risorgimento Crisis," in which Salvatorelli openly denounced Mussolini's regime, equating it with what he liked to call the "anti-Risorgimento."[1]

1. See especially the critical discussion by Alessandro Galante Garrone, "Risorgimento e Antirisorgimento negli scritti di Luigi Salvatorelli," *Rivista storica italiana*, LXXVIII, No. 3 (1966), 513–543; and Walter Maturi, "Luigi Salvatorelli," *Interpretazioni del Risorgimento: Lezioni di storia della storiografia* (Turin: Einaudi, 1962), pp. 550–567.

Vigorously polemical, *Pensiero e azione del Risorgimento* seemed to be the product of a long-smoldering fire that had finally exploded; indeed, the author later revealed to a friend that he wrote his manuscript in the span of but two weeks.[2] At least in the present instance, this can be rated a virtue, for the book represents a condensation of the findings and ideas that Salvatorelli had been either setting down in print or mulling over in solitude for some two decades. Even those who may feel that some of Salvatorelli's arguments are overstated will probably agree that this essay stands out as a minor masterpiece of distillation. It illustrates well the author's conviction that the thought and action of the Risorgimento contained much that was still relevant to a nation about to emerge from the long Fascist night. Since many (though not all) of the interpretations set forth by Salvatorelli have now come largely to be accepted by Italian scholars, it is fitting that his views may now reach a wider audience in this English translation.

Born March 11, 1886, at Marsciano in the province of Perugia, Salvatorelli was graduated from the University of Rome at the age of twenty-one. In the course of his long life (which has now passed the fourscore mark), he was to publish more than thirty volumes and a staggering number of articles and book reviews.[3] This immense scholarly output may be divided into three major categories: the history of Christianity and relations between Church and state; the history of international politics since the Napoleonic era; and the history of Italy in virtually all of its aspects and periods. Seldom, however, was Salvatorelli's research rigidly compartmentalized; there was constant interpenetration of interests and moral judgments. Some thirty years ago, the author explained this connection when he casually described himself as "a modest Italian scholar who today has turned predominantly to themes

2. Cf. the recollections of Alessandro Galante Garrone in *La Stampa* (Turin), December 31, 1963.

3. For a partial listing of them, see Giorgio Levi della Vida, "Salvatorelli storico," *Tempo Presente*, XI, No. 5 (Maggio, 1966), 46–50.

of civil history but who has not forgotten his earlier attachment to the themes of religious history and is conscious of the *moral* link between the two."[4] Though he has been reluctant to state his philosophy of history explicitly, it seems safe to say that Salvatorelli conceived of it primarily as an ethical and political process in which religion was one of the essential aspects. His "ethical-political" outlook led him to regard the Risorgimento as having enduring significance for the contemporary world. Like so many other Italian practitioners of the idealist school of historiography, Salvatorelli was more concerned with the importance of political ideologies than with economic factors. In much of his writing, one also sees a deliberate effort to ask whether things might not have gone differently if there had only been on the part of the leaders a little more farsightedness, moral courage, or constructive determination.

Salvatorelli's first publication was an essay dealing with the manner in which political and social problems were reflected in the religious conscience of Judaism and early Christianity.[5] Thereafter the young university scholar, whose political orientation was that of a liberal monarchist in the style of Giovanni Giolitti, rapidly became interested in the contemporary political and religious situation and drifted into what was to become his other important vocation, journalism. Thus as early as the Balkan Wars of 1912–13 he was contributing articles on foreign policy to *La Tribuna* (Rome) and Cesare De Lollis's review, *Italia nostra*. When the Great War broke out in 1914, Salvatorelli, like Giolitti, argued that Italy should remain neutral rather than fight Austria. The collapse of the Hapsburg Empire, he argued, would open the way for the emergence of a large Yugoslav kingdom, and such a new state would damage Italy's interests in the Balkans and Adriatic as well as kindle

4. Quoted in *ibid.*, p. 46.
5. "Lo Stato e la vita sociale nella coscienza religiosa d'Israele e del Cristianesimo antico," *Studi storici*, XXI, No. 3/4 (1913), 365–428.

Irredentist agitation at home.[6] From 1914 on, Salvatorelli contributed analytical pieces to *Il Tempo* (Rome), *Il Resto del
Carlino* (Bologna), and most often of all to Turin's *La
Stampa*, a highly respected newspaper that enjoyed circulation
throughout Italy.

Salvatorelli did not let his penchant for journalism prevent
him from pursuing his investigations of Church history, studies
which often revealed his harsh opinion of the Church as a
politically authoritarian institution. In 1915, he won a chair in
this field at the University of Naples. But Italy's intervention
in the war that same year quickly interfered, and the young
professor obediently spent the next three years at the front. In
1920, when he was offered the opportunity to become co-
director of *La Stampa*, he had to make the difficult choice of
sacrificing his university chair for a career in journalism. He
opted for the latter.[7] The decision caused almost no scandal,
for in the first quarter of the century very few snobbish barriers existed between Italian academicians and the newspaper
world.[8]

Three and a half years of war stirred up waves of political
and social unrest in Italy. Thus Salvatorelli found himself engaged in the postwar period in a running battle with extremists
on both the Left and the Right, and also in criticism of the
excessively nationalistic atmosphere surrounding the Paris
peace conference.[9] During the months that Mussolini's cudgel-
wielding Fascists were blustering their way to power in 1922

6. Mario Vinciguerra, "Il gruppo della *Italia nostra*, 1914–1915," *Studi
politici*, Serie II, Anno IV, No. 4 (Ott.–Dic., 1957), 657.

7. His departure from the University of Naples opened the chair to another
liberal scholar, Adolfo Omodeo, whose distinguished career resembled that
of Salvatorelli in that he, too, divided his interests between the history of the
Church and the Risorgimento and went through a similar political evolution
during the Fascist dictatorship.

8. Maturi, *Interpretazioni del Risorgimento*, p. 551.

9. His reminiscences of those newspaper battles are set forth in P. Permoli
(ed.), *Lezioni sull'antifascismo* (Bari: Laterza, 1960), pp. 33–49; cf. Massimo
Legnani's essay in Brunello Vigezzi (ed.), *1919–1925: Dopoguerra e fascismo:
Politica e stampa in Italia* (Bari: Laterza, 1965), pp. 254–370.

with the approval of King Victor Emmanuel III, Salvatorelli wrote a series of penetrating articles that sought to dissect Italian Fascism. Later these were published in book form under the title *Nazionale fascismo*.[10] His interpretation of that amorphous ideology has now become a landmark in the literature on the subject, and his coining of the label "National-Fascism" even before the merger of the Fascists with the older Nationalist Party is additional evidence of his perspicacity. In his estimation, "National-Fascism" was not just an Italian but a European phenomenon. A mishmash of antiliberal, anticapitalist, anti-internationalist, antidemocratic, and anti-Socialist elements, "National-Fascism" was the postwar political expression of an exasperated conglomeration of returning veterans, landowners, petty bourgeoisie, white-collar workers, and professional people whose outlook was shaped mostly by emotional considerations. Devoid as these Black Shirts were of a clear-cut economic physiognomy or social function of their own, and caught between the pressures of capitalism on the one hand and the proletariat on the other, they denied the Marxian idea of class struggle and substituted for it the myth of the nation. For Salvatorelli, Fascism was a kind of superheated "Garibaldian romanticism," replete with irrational, activist qualities. He predicted that its excessive and anachronistic worship of the nation-state, together with its "economic infantilism," would surely lead to war and destruction of European economic unity.[11]

For a man like Salvatorelli, inspired by deep respect for rational orderliness and carefully considered change, nothing could be more repellent than the vulgar, brutal ideology Mussolini was concocting in cynical and opportunistic fashion. When the Fascists clamped down the totalitarian state (again with the acquiescence of the House of Savoy), it was hardly

10. Turin: P. Gobetti, 1923.

11. See Adriano Tilgher's discussion of Salvatorelli in *Ricognizioni: Profili di scrittori e movimenti spirituali contemporanei italiani* (Rome: Libreria di Scienze e Lettere, 1924), pp. 39–41.

surprising that they forced Salvatorelli to resign from the directorate of *La Stampa* in 1925. Disgusted with both the Fascist regime and its obliging monarchical accomplice, Salvatorelli shifted to republicanism and resolved to write a critical history of the Fascist era as soon as this might be feasible. For the duration of the dictatorship, however, he prudently confined his publications to politically "safe" topics. Some of these were fairly specialized studies—e.g., biographical interpretations of Saint Francis, Saint Benedict, and Constantine the Great;[12] a history of early Latin Christian literature and an analysis of some of the "higher critical" studies of the origins of Christianity;[13] a discerning article on Raffaele Cardinal Lambruschini, one of the most interesting liberal personalities in the Risorgimento;[14] a discussion of Vatican politics since the Great War;[15] and an account of the evolution of the Triple Alliance.[16] Much broader in scope were his thick tomes on the history of medieval Italy and the ensuing era of the communes,[17] to say nothing of his 600-page "concise" history of Italy from prehistoric times.[18] All of these publications

12. *Vita di San Francesco d'Assisi* (Bari: Laterza, 1926) [English translation, *Life of St. Francis of Assisi* (New York: Knopf, 1928)]; *San Benedetto e l'Italia del suo tempo* (Bari: Laterza, 1929), and *Costantino il Grande* (Bari: Laterza, 1929).

13. *Storia della letteratura latina cristiana dalle origini alla metà del VI secolo* (Milan, 1936); and "Da Locke a Reitzenstein: L'indagine delle origini cristiane," *Rivista storica italiana*, XLV, No. 4 (1928), 341–369, XLVI, No. 1–2 (1929), 5–66 [English translation, "From Locke to Reitzenstein: The Historical Investigation of the Origins of Christianity," *Harvard Theological Review*, XXII, No. 4 (October, 1929), 263–369].

14. "La vocazione di Lambruschini," *Pégaso*, IV, No. 6 (Giugno, 1932), 650–668.

15. *La politica della Santa Sede dopo la guerra* (Milan: Ispi, 1937); *Pio XI e la sua eredità spirituale* (Turin: Einaudi, 1939).

16. *La Triplice Alleanza: Storia diplomatica, 1877–1912* (Milan: Ispi, 1939).

17. *L'Italia medievale dalle invasioni barbariche agli inizio del secolo XI* (Milan: Mondadori, 1937); *L'Italia comunale, dal secolo XI alla metà del secolo XIV* (Milan: Mondadori, 1940).

18. *Sommario della storia d'Italia dai tempi preistorici ai nostri giorni* (Turin: Einaudi, 1938) [English translation, *A Concise History of Italy from*

displayed ample evidence of the author's determination to "remain a rationalist in an era of spreading irrationalism."[19]

It was during the difficult years of the dictatorship that Salvatorelli's ideas regarding the Risorgimento matured—some of them obviously stimulated by the research of men like Francesco Ruffini and Adolfo Omodeo on Cavour and Mazzini, and Cesare Spellanzon on the federalist groups. Salvatorelli's major contribution to Risorgimento scholarship was his pioneering investigation of the political thought of a number of intellectuals in the period between 1700 and 1870.[20] Rejecting the notion that there was a clean break between a "rational" eighteenth century and a "romantic" nineteenth century in Italian political thought, he stressed the continuity of Enlightenment themes not only in the work of such positivists as Carlo Cattaneo and Giuseppe Ferrari but in the novels of Alessandro Manzoni, the pamphlets of the "moderates," and the thought of Mazzini and Cavour. Critics have pointed out, however, that the author deliberately omitted references (at least in the first edition) to writers of the Catholic opposition.[21] Gaps there were, but *Il Pensiero politico italiano dal 1700 al 1870* deserves much praise as the first major effort to rediscover the thought of the Italian Enlightenment and to point out how the state was coming to be looked upon as an instrument for augmenting human happiness—a line of historical investigation that has since been carried on brilliantly by Franco Venturi and others. In addition to the above title and the book translated here, Salvatorelli's publications on the Risorgimento included a polemical pamphlet denigrating the House of Savoy and a variety of shorter studies

---

Prehistoric Times to Our Own Day (New York: Oxford University Press, 1940)].

19. Expressed in his review of Ernesto Buonaiuti's *La Chiesa romana*, in *La Cultura*, XII, No. 2 (Aprile-Giugno, 1933), 390.

20. *Il Pensiero politico italiano dal 1700 al 1870* (Turin, Einaudi, 1935; rev. eds., 1941, 1942, 1949).

21. Maturi, *Interpretazioni Risorgimento*, pp. 554–555.

that in many cases were not printed until the postwar era.[22]

In all of these reflections and polemics on the Risorgimento, several typically Salvatorellian contentions and themes stand out:

1. The Risorgimento was both a material and spiritual phenomenon. It must always be viewed as closely linked to the rest of Europe and the great currents of liberalism, nationalism, and democracy. Thus Salvatorelli rightly rejected the popular notion of Fascist writers that the Risorgimento had purely native Italian roots.

2. There has always been a substantial degree of "national unity" among the Italian people, even during the centuries when the peninsula was divided into a great multiplicity of states—a much more dubious argument.

3. The commonplace assertion that the Risorgimento was carried out by only a small elite is an oversimplification; popular currents played a greater role than many think.

4. Contrary to the myth propagated by Francesco Cognasso and "court historians," the House of Savoy was not really committed to the cause of Italian unification until the 1850s. The "artichoke" policy of territorial enlargement of Sardinia-Piedmont must not be confused with the much more complex process of Italian unification.

5. "Modern" laic and liberal man was born in the period of the Enlightenment rather than in the early nineteenth century (as Omodeo had contended); consequently historians should pay more attention to the religious stirrings in the eighteenth century (e.g., anti-Curialism and Jansenism).

6. The French Revolution was of immense importance in triggering popular participation in the Risorgimento, and the moment when eighteenth-century reformism gave way to Jacobinism was particularly significant. Moreover, the three

22. *Casa Savoia nella storia d'Italia* (Rome: "La Cosmopolita," 1945); *Spiriti e figure del Risorgimento* (Florence: Le Monnier, 1961); and *Unità d'Italia: Saggi storici* (Turin: Einaudi, 1961).

years from 1796 to 1799 posed for Italy all of the political and constitutional problems (e.g., federalism vs. centralism) that later were to be confronted again—an observation that has led to considerable new research by historians.

7. The Napoleonic era was a retrogressive period, much less beneficial to Italy than the preceding decade of the French Revolution—a rather unpersuasive argument that probably resulted from Salvatorelli's disgust with Mussolini's idolization of Napoleon Bonaparte.

8. The Risorgimento sought a "new" Italy, not a restoration; it was nothing if not liberal. Hence such clerical and reactionary anti-French currents in the late 1790s as the Sanfedisti and Lazzaroni in Naples cannot be regarded as belonging to the Risorgimento; instead they must be viewed as the first manifestation of what Salvatorelli liked to call the "anti-Risorgimento." For the most part, too, the Restoration era must also be relegated to the anti-Risorgimento. During the first half of the nineteenth century, the "restored" Kingdom of Sardinia-Piedmont was the most reactionary state in the peninsula. Moreover, any neo-Guelphic or pro-papal interpretation of the Risorgimento must also be rejected, for "the Risorgimento was carried out against the papacy and it could not be otherwise," Salvatorelli insisted. "It will be well for anyone who studies Risorgimento history to comprehend this basic truth, in order that he may not, as Saint Paul said, act in vain."[23] In all of this juxtaposing of Risorgimento and anti-Risorgimento, Salvatorelli's penchant for dialectical argument is evident.

9. The revolutionary year of 1848 was of crucial importance not only for Italy but for all of Europe—as Salvatorelli was to make quite clear in 1949 when, on the occasion of the centennial, he devoted an entire book to what he labeled (in the singular) the "European Revolution."[24] It was his contention

23. Salvatorelli, *Spiriti e figure del Risorgimento*, pp. 253–257.
24. *La Rivoluzione Europea, 1848–1849* (Milan-Rome: Rizzoli, 1949).

(probably overstated) that all of the revolutionary movements of 1848 were organically connected and not simply coincidental in time. They were an extension to all Europe of the Great Revolution of 1789, and though full of diversity they shared one common theme, the search for "national democracy." Italy was in the revolutionary vanguard, for the first outburst occurred in Sicily in January, 1848; moreover, it was to be Italian-style "banquets" that overthrew King Louis Philippe in Paris. Why did not France take the leadership of the European ferment? And why did the revolutionary movement fail? The perhaps oversimplified answer of Salvatorelli was that (a) Socialism had undermined the democratic, interclass unity of the nations of Central Europe and Italy and prevented the French Provisional Government from offering assistance, and that (b) national egoisms had divided the peoples. (He could also have added, as Pierre Renouvin has suggested, the personal decisions of men like Czar Nicholas I.)[25] The failure of Europe to solve its nationality problems in 1848–49 in a healthy and democratic manner opened the way for a distorted and exaggerated form of nationalism that put an obstacle in the path of the formation of an "International of the Peoples" and led to the tragedy of two world conflicts, Salvatorelli was convinced.

10. The publication in 1851 of the Abbé Vincenzo Gioberti's book *Del Rinnovamento civile d'Italia* was of great importance, not only in underscoring Gioberti's own switch from a papal to Piedmontese orientation, but in causing King Victor Emmanuel II to realize that he must either aspire to become King of Italy or risk being reduced to the status of "Monssú Savoia." Moreover, it was of considerable influence in democratizing Victor Emmanuel and making him more Garibaldian than Cavour. On this point, Salvatorelli owed much to the research of Omodeo.

25. Pierre Renouvin, "L'historien de 1848," *Rivista storica italiana*, LXXVIII, No. 3 (1966), 471–478.

11. Mazzini's concept of nationalism must be rescued from the clumsy distortions of Fascist writers, for it cannot be separated from his love for freedom and humanity, Salvatorelli argued with good reason. Moreover, Mazzini intended his unified Italy to form a part of a broad federation of Europe.

12. The crux of the Risorgimento, in Salvatorelli's judgment, was the interrelationship of Mazzini and Cavour. The former personified the gadfly, revolutionary and democratic initiative from below; the latter the liberal-monarchical action from above. Though recognizing that the goals of both Mazzini and Cavour "represented equally profound needs" and were "equally necessary in the course of the historical process," Salvatorelli insisted that it would not be correct to say merely that they both worked together "for a result which, unifying their work, transcended them both. This would probably be a fine bit of historicist compromising, but it would be arbitrary. It would be a little poem, a pastoral eclogue, but not history. For in reality, in that struggle there was a victor and a vanquished; Cavour was the victor, Mazzini the vanquished."[26] Thus Salvatorelli rejected the uncritical tendency of "official" historiography to place the "fathers of the nation" on the same plane without taking into account their deep-seated differences.

13. Napoleon III was a far greater figure than the "tyrant" and "traitor" he seemed to Mazzini. (It is interesting to note Salvatorelli's favorable evaluation of Napoleon III in contrast to his negative one of the uncle.) The head of the Second Empire never resigned himself to being a leader of European conservatism; he also wanted to support the healthy principle of nationality, reorganize Europe on a free-trade basis, and raise standards of living. He was at his best when he devised his collaboration with Cavour at Plombières in 1858. The triumph of Napoleon III's initiative from above over Mazzini's

26. Luigi Salvatorelli, *Prima e dopo il Quarantotto* (Turin: De Silva, 1948), p. 189.

from below was the key to the next half century of European history.

14. Ironically, it was Garibaldi who (in spite of his earlier Mazzinian outlook and hostility to Cavour) tipped the scales in favor of Cavour's plan for a plebiscite to ratify extension of the Piedmontese constitution to all of Italy rather than in favor of Mazzini's plan for a democratically elected constituent assembly that would draw up an entirely new instrument of government.

15. Cavour's formula "A free Church in a free state" was one of the noblest concepts he contributed to the Risorgimento. The repudiation of it by Mussolini in the Lateran Pacts of 1929 marked a victory for the anti-Risorgimento.

In the course of 1942, the last full year of the Fascist dictatorship, Salvatorelli met secretly with a cluster of intransigently laic and republican intellectuals to found a new Partito d'Azione, an underground party whose very name recalled the Risorgimento. Inspired by the thought and action of Mazzini and Garibaldi as well as by the ideas of twentieth-century radical democrats and Socialists, the Actionists were led during the Resistance and Liberation era by such men as Ferruccio Parri, Ugo La Malfa, Emilio Lussu, and Salvatorelli. Though the party was more richly endowed with imaginative and headstrong leadership than a mass following, it played an important role in politics for about three years, bitterly denouncing the House of Savoy as the willing accomplice of Fascism, insisting on the separation of Church and state, demanding democratic and socialist reforms, and advocating a postwar federation of Europe.

In December, 1944, six months after the liberation of Rome, Salvatorelli was able to launch and edit an Action Party weekly newspaper, *La Nuova Europa*. It terminated in March, 1946, by which time it was clear that the Action Party was disintegrating, its left wing drifting toward Communism and the more moderate spokesmen (including Salvatorelli) ending up in new democratic-republican formations. About the same time, the sixty-year-old pundit decided to resume his journalistic collaboration with Turin's *La Stampa*. Since then, he has contributed scores of articles to that newspaper on international and domestic politics, interspersed with discussions of historical and cultural topics.

Despite heavy demands upon his time and energy, Salvatorelli has not neglected historical research since the war. A torrent of books, pamphlets, and scholarly articles has continued to pour off the presses. Some are brand-new, others are revisions of earlier studies, while still others are anthologies of articles and book reviews that originally appeared elsewhere.[27] The two books that stand out as the most significant of these postwar publications are the 340-page *La Rivoluzione Europea, 1848–1849*, mention of which has already been made, and the immensely valuable, pioneering study of Italy under the Fascist regime which Salvatorelli wrote in collaboration with the journalist Giovanni Mira, the 1,000-page *Storia d'Italia nel periodo fascista*.[28]

Taken as a whole, Salvatorelli's historical research and writing has been impressive. Even his most polemical pieces have had the merit of provoking useful historical debate. He has attained high recognition not only in Italy where he has been elected to the venerable Accadeima Nazionale dei Lincei, but also abroad as the translations of several of his works and his

27. In the field of Church history, one may note *La Chiesa e il mondo* (Rome: Faro, 1948); "Le idee religiose di Fra Paolo Sarpi," *Atti dell' Accademia Nazionale dei Lincei*, Anno 350, Ser. 8, Vol. 5, pp. 311–360 (Rome, 1953); and *Chiesa e Stato dalla Rivoluzione francese ad oggi* (Florence: La Nuova Italia, 1955).

In the area of general European history, there are *Leggenda e realtà di Napoleone* (Rome: De Silva, 1944; 2nd ed., 1960); *Politica internazionale dal 1871 ad oggi* (Turin: Einaudi, 1946); *Storia del Novecento* (Milan: Mondadori, 1957; 2nd rev. ed., 1964); *Storia d'Europa* (Turin: UTET, 4th ed., 1961); *Miti e storia* (Turin: Einaudi, 1964); in addition to *La Rivoluzione Europea, 1848–1849*.

28. Turin: Einaudi, 1956; rev. ed., 1964. The original version, profusely illustrated, bore the title, *Storia del fascismo: L'Italia dal 1919 al 1945*, and was published in Rome by Edizioni Novissima in 1952.

election to the International Council of the Historical Sciences attest. Undeterred by age, Salvatorelli is still busily engaged in the task of seeking lessons from history and rational under-standing of the past so that it may help to illuminate the new paths that are opening up for Italy and Europe.

CHARLES F. DELZELL

Vanderbilt University
June, 1969

CHAPTER I

The Problem of the Risorgimento

1. *The Material Conception and the Spiritual Conception*

What does the phrase "the Italian Risorgimento" mean, and above all what is it that "resurges"? In what relation does the Risorgimento stand to modern European history, of which it is the Italian manifestation? To what extent is it a political, an ethical, or a cultural phenomenon? Is it a purely indigenous construct, or does it contain foreign elements and influences? If so, of what kind and in what measure? When does it begin and when does it end? Many of these questions have been treated at length, and many have been resolved, especially in recent times, with affirmations more dogmatic than the solidity of the treatment would warrant. Moreover, these questions have not been examined as a whole, systematically. In that respect, the Risorgimento differs from the Renaissance, which has been discussed a great deal in the last few decades precisely as a total conception. It also differs in that the Renaissance has been treated on the level of European historiography whereas the Risorgimento continues to be considered primarily as a fact of purely Italian interest. Whatever our views may be on this last point, there is no doubt that for us Italians the Risorgimento is a fundamental part of our history, the history of yesterday that projects its shadow on today, the fulcrum of our past and future.

It is interesting to look at the very different interpretations of the various forces at work in the Risorgimento, of their development, and of the results of the Risorgimento itself. At times, these interpretations are so far apart that they completely contradict each other. This is due not only to philosophical differences or to varied historiographical-political orientations, but to contingent political conditions and practical calculations as well. We shall mention just one: the pronounced prevalence of Ghibelline orthodoxy in the period 1870–1914, which was succeeded in the twenty years between the two wars (and in part still continues) by an equally pronounced Guelph tendency, one which may even be called *ancien régime*.

There is an ingenuous conception of the Risorgimento that is broadly and unconsciously diffused. According to it, the Risorgimento consists only of the formation of the Kingdom of Italy, which took place between 1859 and 1861 and was completed in 1866 and 1870. If one accepts such a conception, there is no need to speak of the Risorgimento as a problem; there is nothing to do but rattle off the litany of facts by which the various parts of Italy were aggregated to the Savoyard kingdom of Victor Emmanuel II. There would be nothing but a series of events: battles, military occupations, treaties, plebiscites, parliamentary votes, royal decrees. If we try to discuss this ingenuous conception, it reduces itself to an interpretation of the Risorgimento as a purely political-territorial-state fact. What comes forth is something which on a philosophical plane might be called materialistic positivism, and on a political plane monarchical absolutism.

As a matter of fact, it was maintained in the Fascist period that the process of the Risorgimento consisted in the absorption of the various Italian states or regions of the peninsula by the Savoyard Kingdom of Sardinia. The formation of that kingdom, then, would constitute the prologue—the only prologue—to the new Italy. On the one hand, this thesis is deeply rooted in the conception we have called ingenuous; but on the other, it overcomes and denies that conception itself, inasmuch as it is forced to affirm a central idea, a direction-giving and interpretative criterion. It therefore looks at the Risorgimento not only as a material fact to be purely and simply established and accepted, but as a question to be discussed, a process to be interpreted. The interpretative criterion is said to be the state as a purely authoritarian formation and institution. But the attempt to elevate the ingenuous conception to the level of a sophisticated conception, accomplished by those who for the sake of convenience we shall call the Savoyard school, fails from the beginning; the sophisticated thesis very quickly relapses into ingenuousness. The role played by the Savoyard monarchy in the Risorgimento and the way the role was played are indeed matters of capital importance; but if the Risorgimento consists in the amplification of the Savoyard state into the Kingdom of Italy, it is equivalent to saying that the Risorgimento may be reduced to the addition of the various regions of Italy to Piedmont; that is to say, to the material fact of the annexations. These, in turn, could not be considered as the conclusion of a historical process, nor could they be said to represent the manifestations of the country's will; rather, they are reducible to a pure act of dominion. The national, popular, and intellectual elements in the Risorgimento are denied. No true difference would exist between the formation of Italian unity and any sort of foreign conquest.

We can therefore safely cast aside that ingenuous conception, which reveals itself as intrinsically empty, and we may reject its sophisticated form, though we shall examine its various aspects as we go along. To expose the inconsistencies of the latter form, we will make only two points now. The first is that the territorial or Savoyard conception is incapable of comprehending a range of episodes that indubitably belong to the Risorgimento. If the Risorgimento is reduced purely and simply to the territorial formation of the Savoyard Kingdom of Italy, what place can there be in it for the Neapolitan revolution of 1820 or for the Central Italian revolution of 1831, which simply sought to change the internal structure of some Italian states? The same can be said of the various uprisings in the Romagna between 1840 and 1846, or of those in the Kingdom of Naples between 1821 and 1848. Moreover, all of Mazzini's deeds—aimed toward unification, to be sure, but toward a republican unification—would run the risk of being considered "anti-Risorgimento." (As a matter of fact, that was precisely the ultimate and innermost aim of the men who sustained that theory, one of whom went so far as to speak of "the leprosy of republicanism.") Indeed, even a large part of 1848 and the reform movement immediately preceding it would remain outside the threshold of the Risorgimento. The other consideration is that ever since the term Risorgimento began to be used for a given period of Italian history, and more precisely to indicate the new destinies of our country, it has never been taken in a purely state-territorial sense. From Bettinelli to Carducci, from Alfieri to Gioberti, from the Jacobin patriots to Santarosa, from Mazzini to Cavour, everyone—whether he used the specific term or expressed the idea with other words—everyone has understood the Risorgimento of Italy to be a spiritual fact, or even better a spiritual process, an intimate and complete transformation of Italian life, an affirmation of national and individual autonomy. In fact, the word first had an exclusively or predominantly literary or cultural significance; only later did it assume a political-territorial meaning as well. Italy and the Italian Risorgimento were both understood first and foremost as a fact of conscience, as an act of the spirit.

2. Nova et vetera

The very term "Risorgimento" excludes a purely territorial meaning, which is materialistic under the guise of being political. (And politics is an act of the spirit!) Risorgimento means something that once was there, that has temporarily stopped being there, and then starts again. Now, history knows of no Italian state before the Kingdom of Italy proclaimed in 1861. The so-called Roman-Italian confederation does not deserve the name, for it consisted of a series of bilateral unions between Rome and the various populations of the Italian peninsula, and not of a common political organization. The extension of the right of Roman citizenship to all of Italy after the Social War did not bring about genuinely equal and unified participation of the whole Italian population in the life of the state, for the functioning of political life remained essentially restricted within the city. There was no organic or constitutional link between the municipal Italic autonomies and the central politics of Rome.

With the institution of the Empire and its universalistic-absolutistic evolution, the beginnings of an Italian state were frustrated, and the citizen state became the imperial state. The whole of Italy remained part of the Roman Empire (dependent upon Constantinople in the final period) up to the invasion of Alboin, when it was then divided into two parts, Byzantine Italy and Lombard Italy. In neither did the people play a part in political management: they were, as the phrase goes, the objects and not the subjects of history. The Kingdom of Italy, a continuation of the Lombard kingdom, was subordinated to the new Eastern empire; it never legally—much less factually—comprehended the whole of Italy. In view of its political and social organization, that kingdom must be considered an imposition, over several centuries, of a number of foreign feudatories on the Italian population; it cannot be considered an Italian state.

The Italian people first began to govern themselves in the communes, which appeared as a variety of autonomous local formations subsisting within the imperial realm, without any political bond among them. Even then, effective communal government did not extend beyond Central Italy. The

Southern kingdom was clearly distinct, though closely connected through political relations. In the South, a series of
foreign dynasties succeeded each other, each of them (except
for the first) maintaining political, dynastic, and governmental
ties with foreign countries. With the fifteenth century, we
have a more definite political order in Italy, with several large
states independent in fact, even if formally subject. (The
Duchy of Milan was an imperial fief; the Kingdom of Naples
a fief of the Church, and so on.) These large states, and a
number of small states beside them, were all completely autonomous. With the start of the sixteenth century, foreign domination begins. Although the personality of the former Italian
states was not completely suppressed, foreign domination
nevertheless extended to a considerable part of the peninsula,
now larger, now smaller, and did in fact exercise a strong
preponderance. It ended with the constitution and completion
of the Kingdom of Italy in 1861; and although it absorbed
many historical elements, that kingdom represents an entirely
new creation.

From the end of the eighteenth century onward, there were
those in Italy who hoped for, invoked, and prophesied the
Risorgimento. Though in diverse ways and with different
means, they all contributed to the importance of the prefix
"ri-" in Risorgimento. Eagerly anticipating the future, they all
looked back at the past. They all dug into the history of Italy
for facts, institutions, and men to serve as example, encour-
agement, warning, preparation. They all sought to take up an
uncompleted work, to tie broken threads: some invoked a
Third Rome (Mazzini); some pointed out that the unifying
thread of Italian history was independence, which had been
obtained, lost, reacquired, lost once again, and now had to be
reacquired once and for all (Balbo); some spoke of a historical
Italian primacy, to be reclaimed and restored (Gioberti); and
if not primacy, then at least an honorable position for Italy,
equal to that of the major European nations. Without doubt,

there were exaggerations, confusions, and illusions in these different conceptions of the Risorgimento; when faced with the facts, one or another part of them proved deficient, as we shall have occasion to see. But we must not, as the saying goes, throw out the baby with the bath; the partial errors must not lead us to reject the nucleus of truth common to these conceptions. For the Italian people, it was not a question of an absolute beginning, but of a rebeginning, for they had a long and great history behind them. That this conviction was one of the operative forces in the Risorgimento is beyond doubt; and even if we want to call it a myth, we must nevertheless take account of it precisely because the Risorgimento is not a merely external fact but a spiritual creation. The past history of Italy, "mythically" interpreted, worked to prepare the history of the future.

We cannot, therefore, accept a purely "modernistic" interpretation of the Risorgimento, according to which the process and its result—the new and unified Italy—are considered as the establishment of something which had never been there before in any form. In other words, the history of Italy does not begin with the Risorgimento; rather, the Risorgimento is one of the main periods of that history. The extreme modernistic conception would be an indisputable truth only if one could accept the Risorgimento as a purely political-territorial conception.

Centuries before the formation of the unified Italian state, there had existed an Italian people. The undeniable political multiplicity of medieval Italy does not mean that the idea and the reality of an Italian nation did not exist then, for we must not confuse the concept of nation with that of state, especially a unified state of the modern type. The nuclei of political life which the Italian cities constituted were not foreign to each other, as are the states of different nations. If we compare the relationships between the Italian communes even when they were at war with each other with relations between

England and France or France and Germany in the same period, the reality of a history (and a political history) of Italy bursts forth irresistibly. The Italian communes knew perfectly well that they belonged to the same nation; above and beyond the particular internal political life of every commune, and beyond the fights between them, there was a unity of blood, language, and culture, of family, economic, and religious life. Moreover, the various cities had identical political problems, and the solutions or attempted solutions in one city were intimately linked to those of other cities. All had to deal with problems of the development and transformation of communal institutions; relations between the different socio-political classes; relations with the Empire and the Church. The political life of Northern and Central Italy presents the same aspect everywhere; we see direct political relations not only between city and city, but between region and region. Events in Lombardy have their repercussions in Tuscany; events in Venetia make themselves felt in Piedmont or in Liguria; the Kingdom of Sicily is intimately associated with the destinies of the rest of Italy. Despite their autonomous development even on seas far from Italy, the great maritime cities are deeply interested in events on the peninsula and often take direct part in them. This tight weave of relationships makes it absolutely impossible to write the history of one great Italian city of that time, or even of a region, without at the same time treating all the others. This is even more true for the period of the lordships and principalities, when just a few major states, continually linked through their policies of friendship or hostility, controlled the destinies of all Italy.

When we pass to the period of foreign domination, that thread of unity is not interrupted; in fact, it becomes stronger, even though the Italian people no longer govern themselves. If it is licit, then, to speak of a history of Italy (and not only of Milan, Florence, or Naples) in the time of the communes and of the lordships and principalities, we have even more reason to speak of it in the period of foreign domination. It was precisely then that Italy as a political whole began to take visible shape; the problem of Italian unity arises in European history, treated for now by the foreign powers, but resolved later by the Italian people in the Risorgimento. In the seventeenth century, the idea of a common destiny of Italy brought forth orations and discourses in prose and verse such as had never been heard before. Some—and they are most numerous —think of a confederation of princes; some already outlined the idea (which then seemed utopian) of a union under the government of one man. Some are against the Spanish predominance and would like to balance it through French intervention; others consider Spanish predominance an assurance of Italian tranquility and harmony; some, very generously, would like to do without any of the foreigners. But there is something common to all the political literature from the time of Charles Emmanuel I to the time of Louis XIV, from Girolamo Muzio, the propounder of an Italian confederation in the second half of the sixteenth century, to Vittorio Siri, who toward the middle of the seventeenth century maintained the necessity of French occupation in Italy to achieve equilibrium; and it is that they all consider Italy a political unity and whole; the common interests and destinies of Italy must be provided for according to one guiding idea, with a plan for political unity.

Still, all this by itself could represent nothing more than political ideology or even rhetorical literature, as in the case of the anonymous "Italian gentleman" who, at the beginning of the seventeenth century, spoke of Italy as the "true and legitimate mistress of the world." But if this political journalism is seen in relation to real events, it takes on another aspect. It was precisely the foreign invasions begun by Charles VIII that contributed to putting the question of Italy as a unified political entity into concrete terms. What started as contests for possession of this or that isolated part of Italy (the Duchy of Milan, the Kingdom of Naples) were transformed quite soon into contests for preponderance in Italy, and then for a general reorganization of the Italian peninsula.

An event of great consequence was the union under one ruler of Milan and Naples, Northern and Southern Italy, a union that lasted until 1734. To find anything similar, we would have to go back to the Lombards and the Goths, for there was nothing like it even in the time of Frederick II, who was an important lord in Lombardy, but not direct ruler. The union of North and South under Spain and then Austria was obviously a great calamity for Italian independence; but it furthered the political unification of the peninsula. The question of independence and the question of unity coincide in their final solution, but not in their development. In any case, the union of Milan and Naples under the same foreign ruler brought about the association of the forces dedicated to liberating the two regions from that ruler. The dukes of Savoy were eying Lombardy; Prince Thomas, also of Savoy, planned to invade Naples for the French and, under Mazarin, got the enterprise under way by attacking the Presidii. Several years earlier, in the time of Victor Amadeus, Thomas's brother, a conspiracy was hatched to get the Kingdom of Naples for the duke and Piedmont for his brother Cardinal Maurice, with the Milanese going to the Duke of Mantua. Every plan to expel the Spaniards necessarily brought with it a general reordering of Italy; that is to say, it posed the political problem of Italian unity.

But if the extreme modernistic interpretation of the Risorgimento is not acceptable—for that matter, it does not seem to me to have been expressly maintained by anyone, for opposition to the "unity of Italian history" means something else— still less acceptable would be a purely "pastist" interpretation. In other words, it would be absurd to consider the Risorgimento as a pure and simple continuation of preceding Italian history, as a process of purely internal evolution without revolution, as a purely autochthonous fact, essentially independent of general European history. To be sure, there is a recommencement, there is a resumption of the past; but there is also a new, subversive element that is much stronger; and it is the attempt to fit Italy into the new European reality that took shape after the Renaissance, for the most part independently of Italy. *Nova et vetera:* though the Italy of the Risorgimento appeals to indigenous traditions, though it aspires to become worthy once again of its great past, it is perfectly conscious that the final goals of these appeals and aspirations must be the reunion and conjunction of Italy on a footing of equality with the rest of Europe, which had progressed on its own. The writers in the period of the Risorgimento agree on this point. Moderates vie with radicals, economists with politicians: some speak of introducing representative government of the English type into Italy, without vainly worrying about originality (Balbo); others maintain that the "Risorgimento" had passed from Italy to Germany with the Reformation, then to France with the Revolution, and that now it had to be returned to Italy (Ferrari); still others insist on the inferiority of Italian culture and economic life compared with other European nations. Mazzini, though very Italian, agrees; his ideal of an Italy that is the protagonist and the director of Europe, a nation-apostle, a nation-Christ, presupposes that Italy will fully accept and assimilate all the progress made by Europe, culminating in the French Revolution. Mazzini believes that every succeeding period of humanity must preserve the values of the preceding period and add new ones: "In every series of syntheses, the last must necessarily comprehend the terms of the former plus its own; therefore the unitary synthesis cannot reject the terms conquered by the preceding synthesis of liberty and equality." Still, his overbearing idealism and his heroic vision of the future did not allow him to see entirely the importance and the difficulty of this inclusion of the preceding conquests in the successive ones, and they induced him to jump over stages. His universalism was such that he could even consider the idea of a national fatherland as a transitory stage, to be accepted realistically, but destined to end in a single organization of all humanity.

3. *Old Italy and New Europe*

We can call the extreme modernistic thesis pure Europeanism; the "pastist" thesis we can call nationalistic. Both are one-sided, but the latter is more erroneous and more fraught with dangers for misunderstanding. The purely Europeanist thesis does not suppress the real data of the Risorgimento, nor does it distort its true process; it merely blocks a complete view. The nationalistic thesis, on the other hand, ignores or falsifies the history of Italy before the Risorgimento—the very history which should provide its most solid foundation. For it is precisely from a study of the continuity between pre-Risorgimento and Risorgimento Italy that the European inspiration bursts forth, the European need to which the Risorgimento responds. The Risorgimento takes up the thread of Italian history precisely inasmuch as it brings Italy back to European civilization, back to the path of European progress from which it had departed when it abandoned the traditions of liberty and universality of thought that had formed its true greatness. The truest form of Italianism went hand in hand with the European spirit. Even the extreme formulations of Gioberti ("primacy") and of Mazzini ("mission") were nothing but manifestations or transformations, though partly disguised, of this European sense that impressed itself upon Italy.

Since it is debatable whether the pre-Roman and Roman periods belong to Italian history or prehistory (though we think that at least at the time of the Social Wars there is a dawn of Italian history), we may leave them aside and say that the life of our people took on a definite form in the twelfth century, when it emerged from the Roman-barbaric-Christian potpourri and from the disarray of feudalism. It happened in the age of the communes and through the work of the communes. Their emergence was accompanied (and at the same time contradicted) by the contemporaneous formation (by no means coincidental) of the Kingdom of Sicily. The period from the end of the eleventh century to the beginning of the sixteenth is the great period of Italian history, the one in which all our economic, political, cultural, moral, and religious energies are fully and harmoniously developed, in which the tenor of life is elevated and refined, in which the forms of the state are complicated and perfected, in which literature, art, and science flourish. This fullness of civilization raises Italy to a higher level than any other European nation. This is the period Bettinelli called the Risorgimento; later it was called the Renaissance, though that term was applied more properly to the fifteenth and sixteenth centuries, which present some distinctive characteristics when compared with the three preceding centuries. There is no need here to get involved in the recent debate concerning the relationship between the two periods—a debate connected with the problem of establishing whether there was opposition or continuity between the Middle Ages and the Renaissance. What is important for us is to take clear cognizance of this period of about four and a half centuries, a period which, from our point of view, can and must be considered unitary.

This period saw the full development of Italian life; in politics, it goes from the blossoming of the communes to the "balance" of the principalities; in philosophy, it goes from the early Scholasticism of Saint Anselm to Ficino and Pico through Saint Thomas Aquinas and Saint Bonaventure; in literature, it goes from the *Cantico delle creature* to *Orlando Furioso*, by way of the *Divine Comedy* and the *Decameron*; in art, it goes from Antelami through the Pisanos, Giotto, and the Florentine fifteenth-century artists up to Michelangelo. A superb, integral, and uninterrupted blossoming of life. We will only note (and it is essential for our purposes) that in the first

part of this period of more than four centuries, Italian civilization unfolds almost entirely within the boundaries of the nation, whereas in the second it spills beyond and Italy becomes
the teacher of Europe. Italian history, though connected with
the rest of Europe, has an autonomous character all the way to
the end of the period. The Italian states are independent; the
Italian people are subjects, not objects, of history, and they
have their destinies in their own hands. This blossoming and
cultural preponderance went together with the autonomous
political personality of the nation; but the cultural-spiritual
moment was superior to the political-territorial.

Everything changed in the course of the sixteenth century:
it is the century of the great Italian crisis, the century of the
transition from the splendors of the Renaissance to the sadness
and flatness of the seventeenth century. With the end of the
Renaissance and the ripening of the Counter-Reformation,
Italian culture lost the position of predominance it had held
for about two centuries in Europe. In the nations beyond the
Alps, particularly in Western Europe, the new cultures, arising
on national soil tilled and made fertile by the civilization of
the Italian Renaissance, began to develop autonomously and
vigorously. Gradually, with the roles reversed, they came to
exercise a pronounced influence on Italian culture. The change
was especially radical in the field of philosophical-scientific
thought. The period of the Counter-Reformation outside Italy
presents positive and negative elements in contrast, with the
former prevailing above all in the two great Western nations,
France and England. Political and religious quarrels goad
men's minds and keep them alert. But in Italy there was the
silence of stagnation: the double burden of Empire and
Church weighed heavily on the peninsula. The imprisonment
of Campanella, the burning of Bruno, and the condemnation
of Galileo mark the extinction of independent thought in
Italy. Our country not only lost intellectual primacy, but even
moved out of the sphere of productive European culture, to

enclose itself in pure erudition and in scholastic logomachies. Modern thought lives and develops outside Italy. Modern philosophy begins with Descartes; when the first signs of a cultural revival appeared in Italy toward the end of the seventeenth century, the philosophical and scientific fields developed for the most part under the influence of Cartesianism. (Even in the field of erudition, other foreigners were our teachers, especially Mabillon and the Benedictines of the French congregation of Saint Maur.) The influence of Descartes was followed by that of Newton; and although there were Italian masters in the field of historical erudition and research at the beginning of the eighteenth century, English and French philosophy hold the scepter in the world of thought.

So much for the field of culture. As for politics, there is no need to waste words to show how low things had sunk. Having lost national independence in the first three decades of the sixteenth century, Italy (as we already pointed out) was in the center of European politics only as a bone of contention in the struggle for preponderance among the great powers who decided its destinies. Even the new political forms—absolute monarchy, constitutional parliamentary monarchy—were developed outside of Italy.

Occasionally, contemporary Italian historiography makes some attempt to re-evaluate the Counter-Reformation and the Italian seventeenth century. Sometimes it is done in the field of art, accentuating the positive elements in the baroque, exalting all its representatives, and rediscovering now and then some hitherto ignored genius. Sometimes it is done in politics, recounting for the nth time the virtues of Charles Emmanuel I ("champion of Italian independence"), or presenting the Medicean principality as a precursor of the modern state, or making an apologia for Spanish domination (an apologia which reduces itself to showing that the devil is not as ugly as he is made out to be). Sometimes—and this is the most frequent case—the attempt is made in the field of religion, exalting the merits of the Roman Inquisition for having maintained the religious unity of Italy and for having saved it from heresy. But the attempt fails to make the obvious and fundamental distinction between a spontaneous, living religious unity and a uniformity imposed from without; it does not ask what profound results the Italian Counter-Reformation had for the life of the spirit and for the religious consciousness; it fails to make any comparison with the very different state of things in France, where Catholic religious life in the same period was far richer and had more inner vitality. These defenses of the Counter-Reformation are simple illusions, easily dispelled by the obvious reality of the spiritual, political, and economic decadence of Italy in the period. The enormous proportions of that reality are revealed if we compare it with the earlier state of Italy, and with the contemporary state of other European nations.

The facts are unshakable and incontrovertible: the line of Italian life ascended from 1100 to 1300, remained at a high level (though not without partial descents) up to the sixteenth century, then declined precipitously from 1530 to the end of the century, to remain in the depths throughout the entire seventeenth century. So far as politics is concerned, it is futile to discuss the greater or lesser wisdom of this or that ruler's projects, just as it is futile to emphasize the conflicts between the Savoyard princes and the foreign rulers of Italy, or to exaggerate the expressions of Italian independence in the seventeenth century. What counts is that those conflicts, those expressions, and in fact all of political life lacked participation by the people (and people here includes the upper classes). What counts is that the consequences were indifference, mis-education, and the calcification and impoverishment of the ruling classes, all of which went together with the dominant fact of subjugation to foreign dominion. So far as culture is concerned, a variegated and abundant harvest of erudition and fleeting flashes of personality do not make up for the absence of a true intellectual life. As for religion, the appreciable individual and social value of a faith sincerely professed and of moral customs observed (or at least recognized) cannot hide the boredom of passively repeated formulas; nor can it conceal the exhaustion of the inner light irradiated by religion in preceding centuries, when it transformed and elevated daily life. The common feature of the period is the lowering of the vital tone: the various elements of national life are dissociated from one another, so that politics is reduced to reason of state, culture to professional erudition or to the caprice of the virtuosi, and religion to formal observance of traditional and obligatory ritual.

In Italy's three great sister nations, France, England, and Germany (which like Italy had emerged from an elaboration and transformation of medieval individualism and universalism), political, economic, and cultural evolution went ahead hand in hand with religious changes and struggles, for a period of one and a half centuries. In fact, the religious element is the dominant and unifying one, so much so that even the textbooks of history duly refer to this as the period of the Wars of Religion. The religious problem remained in the limelight even after the wars. After the Peace of Westphalia, the English Revolution, and the withdrawal of the Edict of Nantes, there were the problems of Jansenism and the Jesuits in France, and Deism and Rationalism (the so-called Enlightenment) in England, France, and to a lesser degree in Germany. The final consolidation of Protestantism in Germany, in the face of the Counter-Reformation, and the move toward religious freedom go along with the disintegration of the Holy Roman Empire and the development of the German states, whose union was later to bring about German national unity. In France, the severe restrictions on Protestantism, the official establishment of "Gallican liberties," and the repression of Jansenism are all closely connected with royal omnipotence and with centraliza-tion of the state; these, in turn, produced the *philosophes* and the Revolution, which represent at once a reaction and a direct development. Pascal and Bossuet, the princes of French prose, were also masters of moral and theological doctrine: *mutatis mutandis,* the same can be said of Voltaire and Rousseau. In England, there is an even more obvious connection between constitutional and social development on the one hand and the religious wars on the other, as there is between the philosophy of Locke and Deism. To formulate the matter synthetically, we can say that in modern France, England, and Germany, and especially in the first two, a profound moral unity permeated the various aspects of life and the various activities of the spirit.

Italy had known such moral unity. In the thirteenth and the fourteenth centuries, art and thought were bound together with political and religious life in a very strong union of sentiments and energies. The *Divine Comedy* is the supreme artistic expression of the young Italian people, the mirror of the political discussions and struggles of the time, the scientific and religious encyclopedia of the mature Middle Ages. Giotto does not paint for himself, for a particular clientele, or for a conventicle; he paints for an entire people taught and comforted not only by the details of the life of Christ, but also by those of his great imitator, the religious hero of the Italian people. In the fifteenth century, the unity begins to loosen: the scholars of the Renaissance are much farther away from the people than Dante and Saint Bonaventure had been. An aesthetic tendency begins in literature and art. Later, the unity clearly falls apart. In the sixteenth century, Italy was invaded and tormented and passed from one hand to another; its great artists witnessed the agony and the death of national independence, the condemnation of Luther, and the Council of Trent; but their artistic world of lines and colors fails to reflect the reality that surrounds them. During the supreme moral and political crisis of Italy, the greatest work of poetry is nothing but one long *divertimento,* a great, hearty laugh. Michelangelo felt within him all the conflicts and torments of his age, but all he expressed of them was the closed and impotent anger of his individual soul. Finally, the spiritual break is complete. Art becomes aestheticism and rhetoric; science (though more slowly and touching great heights on the way) becomes professional technics; religion becomes external and habitual confessionalism.

Taking the word "religion" in its profound sense, it is the unity of moral life that determines the religious character of a people. The cause and the significance of the fact that the Reformation did not succeed in Italy has been discussed at length: some have given a negative value to that fact and some a positive, according to their individual persuasions, their militant convictions, or simply because of fashion, convenience, or easy opportunism. But the absence of a Reformation in Italy is an effect, not a cause. The essential point is not that Italy did not become Protestant, but that, faced with the great religious crisis, it remained indifferent as a nation. Religiosity had already become an individual affair; religious observance had become social behavior. Below the level of superficial and hypocritical harmony, dividing lines had arisen between religion, morality, and politics. That is why the Italian people did not react to the Reformation, neither absorbing it nor transforming it, nor voluntarily and consciously rejecting it. The Counter-Reformation in Italy was essentially an authoritarian superstructure raised over indifferent individual consciences, a baroque decoration covering the religious and moral void.

The dissociative crisis in Italian moral life, which came to a head in the Counter-Reformation and the seventeenth century, had already begun, as we suggested, in the Renaissance. Compared with the organicity of moral life in Italy in the age of the communes, the Renaissance looks like a period of spiritual crisis, to which several great artists, from Botticelli to

Michelangelo, gave poignant expression. In Renaissance Italy, medieval faith and the traditional conception of life and the world were shaken; but the new, self-assured human faith was not yet attained—nor would it be until the eighteenth century. Above all, the spiritual liberation of the individual, an imperfect thing in any case, was not fitted into the new social conception and organization. The individual felt he was without moral support, suspended in midair. This state of things inspired some men with a sense of limitless affirmation and dominating egotism (as in the case of the Renaissance tyrants or Cesare Borgia); but it made others, who were morally better but weak and uncertain, withdraw into themselves and suffer from bewilderment, solitude, and nostalgia (the sick melancholy of Botticelli, the crepuscular ecstasy of Giorgione).

The political crisis of the Italian nation goes hand in hand with the moral crisis of the individual. The division of Italy into various states and the discordant and egotistical foreign policy of those states have been used too insistently to explain the catastrophe of Italian independence at the beginning of the sixteenth century. We must bring more attention to bear on the lack of maturity and of organic structure in each of those states. There was no true fusion of the various cities and of the various classes, nor was there a solid and profound administrative structure, a collective political life, a popular political conscience—in a word, there was no adequate moral base. The people were present in the communes, but absent in the principalities. Public order and material prosperity had increased, but the inner vitality nourished by the communal struggles had decreased. So far as the "Italian tragedy" is concerned, the key to foreign policy is to be found in domestic policy. To a great extent, the Italian principalities, including Medicean Florence, kept their character of improvisation by force, skill, and luck, without having a true political-moral basis either in divine right, in the traditional prestige of an ancient dynasty, or in the popular will freely and organically expressed. The imperial and papal investitures were mere legal formalities without any real effect on the consciences of princes or peoples. With the people absent from public life, the administration of the state became a purely professional matter for the prince and his functionaries.

Savonarola reacted against that moral dissociation: his great significance in Italian history is that he felt the crisis and tried to overcome it. Savonarola tried to bring morality back to public and private life through a religious revival, and to sanctify politics as the work of God. After him (separated not only by time) we must remember Paolo Sarpi, who was not just a political man and a jurist, as he is made out to be most of the time. Neither was his chronological and intellectual successor Pietro Giannone. Sarpi and Giannone had religious interests, too, though there is great difference between their scientific and political cast of mind and Savonarola's prophetic bent. Their battles against the Roman Curia contained a religious motive, the sincerity of which there is no reason to doubt, whatever one may think of the intrinsic historical or theological value of their theses. Both believed that the Roman Church of their day had degenerated from the original Christian Church; the Roman Church had altered Christ's institutions, transforming them from things spiritual, moral, and religious into things temporal, juridical, and political. That is the fundamental concept both of the *History of the Council of Trent* and of the "Papal Reign" of Giannone, the third part of the *Triregno*. They are not concerned simply with juridical theses in favor of the state, but with an organic conception of the Church and of Christian religion. The point of the controversy is essentially religious, and they mean to fight in the name of the Gospel and in its interests.

Giannone speaks with accents of lively scorn when he talks of the degeneration and paganizing of the Church, which he pursues even into strictly religious areas, such as the cult of saints and the doctrine of transubstantiation. Sarpi forcefully asserts that the defense of the state against what he calls clerical usurpation is a matter of supreme importance to religion precisely because it means fighting against the fundamental degeneration and secularization of the Church. It is well known that Sarpi has been accused (precisely by the most orthodox writers) of covert Protestantism. Without trying to resolve that question now (the first step in which would be to define terms exactly), we can safely say that his ideas go well beyond the political-ecclesiastical realm, to reach a purely religious ground. Even if we do not take into account his discussion of the questions of justification by faith and predestination, it will suffice to recall his notion of the Church as a community of believers, rather than a hierarchical ecclesiastical organization—a notion that has religious implications of vast importance. There is more: this supposedly purely political man was devoted to the idea that the divine will is continually acting in history, and with its sovereign power determines the course of events regardless of human design or wisdom. In its passive resignation, his religiosity is quite different from that of Savonarola; but it is nonetheless true and profound religiosity.

Between Savonarola and Sarpi, we might insert those who have recently been called "Italian heretics" (Curione, Gribaldi, Gentile, Ochino, and the two Sozzinis). The word "heretic" here must be taken not in the usual sense, but in the sense of rebels not only against the old Catholic Church but also against the new Protestant churches, and against orthodoxy in general. Undoubtedly, the direct passage from humanism to the modern world is to be found in the Italian heretics: compared with them, the Protestant churches represent a sort of great "detour," but one that was historically necessary and had religious and social value. Passing through the division in the Catholic Church brought about by Protestantism, this current later flowed into eighteenth-century Deism and Rationalism, and generated the modern world founded on liberty of thought and conscience, on reason, and on individual morality. The historical importance of these Italian heretics thus appears to be truly of the first order. It is noted here not with any anti-Catholic apologetic intention (as some people wrongly thought, either out of carelessness or unpreparedness, when I expressed this judgment elsewhere); it is simply a matter of objective history of ideas and intellectual currents. The importance of these "Italian heretics" is one of the least noticed and most important contributions of Italy to Europe, in the tradition of the Renaissance. It does not represent a harbinger of the cultural and moral awakening of Italy at the beginning of the Risorgimento, for Italy was precisely the nation least influenced by the "Italian heretics." The revival of the religious problem (which is fundamental in the history of a people) takes place in Italy in the eighteenth century, and proceeds along completely different paths, with an alliance between anticurialism and Jansenism.

CHAPTER II

The Eighteenth Century

1. Political Data and Historical Realities

Everyone agrees nowadays that the beginnings of the Risorgimento must be moved back from 1815 to the eighteenth century. Even a quarter of a century ago, when the first volume of Raulich's *History of the Risorgimento* appeared, it made an anachronistic impression because it began with the old date. In Carducci's study *On the Italian Risorgimento*, written in 1895 as the introduction to his *Lectures on the Risorgimento*, he gives the date 1748 as the terminus of the pre-Risorgimento period. It was a political date (the Treaty of Aix-la-Chapelle); but Carducci gave it a very much wider sense by saying that in the second half of the eighteenth century the old Italian society had begun to disappear to make room for a new order of things. On the other hand, another current of thought has insisted on the purely political factors, pointing out the reduction to a minimum of foreign dominion in Italy (only in Milan and Mantua) through the Treaty of Aix-la-Chapelle, and the aggrandizement of Piedmont. But the purely political conception (which should be called political-territorial) celebrates its triumph—one might even say its Saturnalia—with another date, 1713 (the Peace of Utrecht), a date that came into vogue chiefly during the last years of Fascism. As a matter of fact, several years ago I too attributed more importance to that date than it really merits.

The political tendency implicit in the choice of that date is different from the one behind the choice of 1748. For the latter, we may speak of a federalistic conception, inasmuch as it points to the fact that after the Treaty of Aix-la-Chapelle Italy found itself almost completely under its own rulers, returning therefore to a situation similar to that before 1494, when the foreign invasions began. The date 1713, on the other hand, emphasizes Savoy and unity. It sees in the Peace of Utrecht above all the aggrandizement and the heightened preeminence in Italy of the House of Savoy, which now achieved a royal crown. Both dates have the intention of pushing the process of the Risorgimento back to a time before the French Revolution, and of portraying it as more or less independent of the Revolution.

As we have seen in Carducci, the date 1748 is capable of including a broad interpretation of the beginnings of the Risorgimento; politics and culture, reform and philosophy can all be associated through it. The Risorgimento would then appear to be a movement of ideas, a sociopolitical transformation before it becomes a territorial-political innovation. It is only in this large sense that the date 1748 has true value from the point of view of the Risorgimento, whereas it becomes rather insignificant if we limit ourselves to considering the new political-territorial structure of Italy after the Treaty of Aix-la-Chapelle. We have already taken note of the remarkable similarity between that structure and the political arrangement of Italy after the Peace of Lodi (1454). One of the most important elements of the similarity is precisely the lack of solidity in each of the structures: in both cases, the collapse came in less than half a century. Seen purely from the viewpoint of the national state, the French invasion of 1796 was no less a catastrophe (or the beginning of a catastrophe) than the invasion of 1494. But even the most obdurate Sanfedisti would find it very hard to deny that the revolutionary period begun in 1796 has a positive relationship to the Risorgimento, whereas the period begun in 1494 ends ineluctably with the loss of Italian independence and with the moral and political debasement of our country. Now, to resolve the apparent contradiction contained in attributing a positive effect to foreign domination and to the demolition of the indigenous states (including Savoy), one must rise above the viewpoint of the national state.

The year 1713, with the Peace of Utrecht, brought about two political-territorial innovations in Italy: the substitution of Austria for Spain in Lombardy and in the South, and the elevation of the House of Savoy to royalty, together with the enlargement of its dominions. From the viewpoint of the national state, the first innovation ought to be considered negative, a liability, for the government of Austria was superior to that of Spain, and more capable of conciliating and winning over its subjects. Moreover, the new rulers in Lombardy were all the stronger because of the vicinity of the Hapsburg states. The supporters of the date 1713, therefore, stress the second innovation. Their interpretation of the Risorgimento is the one which we have called "Savoyard" precisely because it considers the Risorgimento summarized in and resolved through the amplification of the Savoyard state from Piedmont to all of Italy.

Those who associate that date with this conception quickly run into a very grave difficulty. The acquisition of the Kingdom of Sicily by Victor Amadeus II could appear to be a beginning of Savoyard hegemony in the entire peninsula; Victor Amadeus would press from the two extremes, north and south, as though to anticipate 1860. There is no need to discuss what is real and what is only apparent or fantastic in such a presentation: the point is that this new beginning lasted *l'espace d'un matin*. By 1720, Victor Amadeus II had to give up Sicily, in consequence of a blow struck by Alberoni for Spanish revenge, and had to be satisfied with Sardinia in exchange, which was not only smaller and less important, but also did not have the dominant or impressive geographical position which we have seen was true of Sicily. It was not really an exchange but almost a dethronement. The possession of Sardinia had no importance whatever for the later destinies of Savoy and Italy, unless it be that the dynasty took refuge there during the Napoleonic period under the protection of an English fleet, much as the Bourbons took up quarters in Sicily. The rapidity of the exchange, which took place through the Olympian raising of an eyebrow by the great powers, shows just how little Savoy counted in the international game of politics.

In the second decade of the eighteenth century, Savoy failed to achieve its major political-territorial objective, the acquisition of Lombardy, though it rounded itself out locally and made some eccentric acquisitions of dubious value. In the wars of the Polish and Austrian successions, it again had to be satisfied with local rounding out instead of its major objective. At the end of the half century following the Treaty of Aix-la-Chapelle, we find that the Hapsburg Empire had taken over Milan and Mantua as its fiefs and reaffirmed its *de facto* power over Parma and Piacenza, over Tuscany, and over Italian affairs generally, whereas Piedmont had made only modest local gains. As a matter of fact, the emperor himself governed in Tuscany (though through a separate government), and was succeeded by a member of the imperial family. The Republic of Venice by this time had no influence at all in Italian affairs, and neither the desire nor the ability to contest or counterbalance foreign powers. (Indeed, its own territory had been violated by the belligerents with impunity.) This was even more true of the Papal States, which had lost even the last scraps of political importance. In the Kingdom of Naples (as in Parma and Piacenza), close dynastic links made the new dynasty look to Spain and follow its directives. Finally, the main fact was that indigenous forces took almost no part in determining the changes that took place in Italy. Once again, the destinies of the peninsula had been decided by foreign powers, who had made Italy their battlefield. In conclusion: the political-territorial results of the first half of the eighteenth century in Italy do not have nearly the great importance for the process of the Risorgimento that many people believe, or pretend to believe.

2. The Savoyard Myth

Those who favor the date 1713 for the reasons we know start out with the ingenuous presupposition that because the Piedmontese-Savoyard state is the most important element at the conclusion of the Risorgimento (which, as we know, they see only as a political-territorial phenomenon), it must also be in the same dominant position at the beginning. The centrality of Piedmont in the history of Italy from 1859 to 1861 is anticipated and projected backward. The year 1713 is not the terminus of the backward projection, but only one of its principal stages. From Victor Amadeus II, first king of Sardinia, they go back naturally to Charles Emmanuel I, champion of Italian independence ("Charles, that generous, undaunted heart" and all that goes with it), and from him to Emmanuel Philibert, who reconstructed the state of Savoy. From Cateau-Cambrésis, they jump to the fourteenth and fifteenth centuries (since this thesis can find absolutely nothing to do in the first half of the sixteenth century) to show that even then Savoyard Piedmont was already of primary importance in the history of Italy. With this we are in the realm of political myth, a myth that was created in the final period of the Risorgimento, was systematized, and became official doctrine especially in elementary and secondary school teaching in the post-Risorgimento. Then it was taken up again in the Fascist period, with doctrinaire (statist) accents, and used with virulent hostility against all the traditions and values of the Risorgimento, putting Charles Albert of 1833 in the place of Mazzini, and General Galateri in the place of Andrea Vochieri.

Political myths are understandable and justified in the field of action, propaganda, and free political struggle; but history is something else. And history says that up to the second half of the sixteenth century (the most important period in Italian history, from the communes to the Renaissance) Savoy had practically no importance in the general political life of Italy. Savoy played no role whatever in relations among the principalities and in their system of "balance of power," which attained its most complete form in the middle of the fifteenth century. The fantastic role attributed to Savoy, that of being the "guardian of the gates of Italy," was surely not carried out during the period of the foreign invasions. Even Galeani Napione, who was so very Piedmontese and Savoyard, admitted that Charles VIII had come through to conquer the Kingdom of Naples "with the help of our princes." Later, at the end of one of the many futile wars of Charles Emmanuel I, it was precisely the duke of Savoy who opened those gates by ceding Pinerolo to France in the Treaty of Cherasco.

The territorial reconstruction of the state by Emmanuel Philibert does honor to the tenacity and sagacity of that prince; but it was an effect of the equilibrium that had been established between France and Spain, and it in no way substantially modified the servitude of Italy in the Spanish period. The policy of Charles Emmanuel I, celebrated as an affirmation of independent nationality, was above all a desire for aggrandizement in any direction, toward France and Switzerland as much as toward Italy. The program of union between Lombardy and Piedmont was an expedient of Henry IV and of French policy generally even more than it was a guiding idea of the House of Savoy. For a half century following the death of Victor Amadeus I in 1637, Savoy, reduced to dependence on France, went through an almost total eclipse. In the European wars that lasted from the end of the seventeenth to the middle of the eighteenth century, Piedmont—and here we can repeat what we said of Emmanuel Philibert—maintained itself with tenacity and sagacity, recovered its autonomy, brought about territorial gains, and achieved the royal crown; but it was unable to replace the foreign rulers in Lombardy, and it was unable to make any substantial change in the inferior political position of Italy. In the forty years from 1749 to 1789, Piedmont underwent another partial loss of authority because of the agreement between Austria and France, which removed the main basis of its active foreign policy.

Because of the Savoyard myth, perfectly analogous episodes in Italian history have been given completely different meaning, depending on whether they dealt with Piedmont or with another state. The designs of the House of Savoy on Genoa were not very different from and in no way more idealistic than those, let us say, of Austria and Spain on the Valtellina. The conspiracies of Vachero and Della Torre against Genoa, in which both the first and the second Charles Emmanuel played an unfortunate role, were no more worthy than the conspiracy of Bedmar against Venice, behind which there was supposed to be the hand of Spain. The absorption of Montferrat by Savoy was an event not substantially different from the absorption of Ferrara and Urbino by the Pope. Charles Emmanuel I worked against European equilibrium and to the detriment of Italy by following the lead of Philip II, the head of the Counter-Reformation, and pouncing on the prey in France, which was then being torn apart by the Wars of Religion; Ferdinand I of Tuscany and Sixtus V, on the other hand, pursued a more Italian policy. And the man who posed as the champion of Italian independence against the Hapsburgs in about 1615 was the same man who, a dozen years later, sided with them in the war of succession in Montferrat. He even incurred the shame of being among the authors of the sack of Mantua, an event that extinguished one of the centers of Italian culture.

In sum: the policy of Savoy up to the French Revolution was the policy of a third-class state that tried by any means to maintain and enlarge itself, and succeeded in passing from third- to second-class status. The tenacity, political art, and military force behind that work have been justly admired, but we do not see any particular connection to a national policy, except for a very distant one; namely, that all this will have been useful once Piedmont did decide to pursue such a policy. For the time being, Piedmont did nothing of the sort. The ascending line of the Risorgimento, as we shall now see, follows a completely different trajectory: the line of cultural renovation and internal reform, in which Piedmont (especially the Piedmontese government) does not play a leading or even considerable part.

3. The Intellectual Risorgimento of the Eighteenth Century

The Savoyard thesis tries to shift the significance of the eighteenth century in Italian history and the Risorgimento by moving it from the realm of reform and culture to the realm of the territorial state. But it is a vain attempt, made against the eloquence of the facts and the unanimity of the Risorgimento tradition. Throughout the course of the eighteenth century, all of Italian life was concentrated on reform and culture. In the second half of the century, before the Revolution, no one in Italy thought of throwing the Austrians out of Lombardy; and the Bourbon kingdom governed by Tanucci received from Madrid the dictum of Charles III, "*in quo vivimus, movemur et sumus*," which the Abbé Galiani wrote to Tanucci himself. The territorial configuration of the peninsula is considered stable, definitive; and during that long era of peace, minds turn toward celebrating the superiority of modern times and modern governments over the ancients. (See, for instance, Muratori's conclusion to his *Annali*.) This feeling of superiority is based on the reforms carried out by the various governments, especially by the Austrians in Lombardy, by the House of Lorraine in Tuscany (which was also under Austrian princes), and by the Spanish Bourbons in Naples. The old states, those which could historically most justifiedly be called national or indigenous, are now second-rate (Piedmont) or simply do not count at all (Venice, Genoa, the Papal States). Observations such as these make it very hard to defend the thesis of a purely autochthonous, aboriginal Risorgimento. But let us get to the heart of the question, which resides in the nature of the reform.

We can say that its essential characteristics are: antifeudalism, most of all in Lombardy, least of all in Naples; uniform and centralized administrative organization, to supersede legislative and institutional chaos and the stratifications caused by traditions of privilege; anticlericalism—or, rather, anti-Curialism—i.e., the attempt to reduce the power of the Church (more specifically, of the pope) and strengthen the power of the state; hints at ecclesiastical reform, which toward the end of the period developed in the direction we all know (Scipione de'Ricci and the Pistoian Synod); religious tolerance and the incipient secularization of the state and social life; humanitarianism, manifesting itself in the softening of the penal law and culminating in the abolition of capital punishment under Leopold. They are more or less the same characteristics we find embodied in the reforms carried out by other European states. All of this was simply the application of the principles of philosophy and rationalism, formulated in England between the end of the seventeenth century and the beginning of the eighteenth, then passed over to France (which became their bastion with Voltaire and the Encyclopedists), and later propagated in Germany, Italy, and the rest of Europe. So far as the institution of reforms is concerned, Italy holds a very honorable place with Bernardo Tanucci and with Peter Leopold and his excellent co-adjustors. It holds an equally honorable place in the field of ideas: Italian writers are rather timid in philosophy and religion, though their work is indeed impregnated with rationalism and sensism; but they are a great deal more daring in the fields of economics and administration. Their work is characterized especially by the new conception of politics (which already glimmered quite perceptibly in the *Annali* of Muratori), leaving behind the old *ragion di stato* in favor of social utility and the liberation and elevation of the individual. But this Italian movement, both theoretically and practically, is plainly European: it is brought to Italy from abroad, by the foreign reformer-princes (who were, though, vigorously aided by their native ministers). Above all, it is a result of the diffusion of the science, the philosophy, and the *Weltanschauung* of countries beyond the Alps.

The attempt to find in Italian eighteenth-century thought an originality based on its uniqueness or on its opposition to contemporary thought is thoroughly futile and is done either out of intellectual prejudice or for practical ends. Naturally, we are speaking of Italian thinkers who count—Beccaria, Filangieri, Verri, and others like them. No weight can be given to the erudite and trivial academic works written by "right-minded men," who have never counted for anything in the history of thought. (It is rather comical to speak of those Piedmontese "lovers of country" who opposed "their own history, the Savoyard tradition, themselves" to Montesquieu, Rousseau, Diderot, Condillac, Voltaire.) More importance can be attached to some of Goldoni's witty quips against the traditional arrogance and corrupting influence of the nobility, and in favor of the bourgeoisie and the working people, than to those erudite trivia.

Philosophy and reason are the goddesses of Italian eighteenth-century thought, just as they are of English, French, and German thought; and from England and France, at least, the Italians learned much. Italy gets its ideas from beyond the Alps, assimilates them, and strengthens them with its own sap, stimulated by the graft of foreign ideas. Italy of the eighteenth century takes up the broken thread of its tradition: the Risorgimento derives from the Renaissance. But the derivation is not direct, nor does it take place on the nation's own soil; it is accomplished through Europe. After being isolated throughout the Counter-Reformation and the seventeenth century, Italy rejoins Europe and thereby begins to find itself.

4. *The Revival of the Religious Problem*

We can see it particularly well in the ecclesiastical-religious realm. A little earlier, we treated Savonarola, Sarpi, and Giannone together, showing how they form an indigenous chain in a tradition of religious reform that stretches across two and a half centuries. But Savonarola and Sarpi remained isolated and ultimately impotent: the former ended on the scaffold, with the approval of the papal legate; the latter was barely able to escape the attempts made on him by the Curia. Nor was Giannone much more fortunate, for he died after a long imprisonment in Savoy, where he had been lured and then held in order to please the court of Rome. But while he was dying in jail, his ideas were beginning to have success. Those ideas were being carried to a level higher than the purely juridical level to which he restricted himself in the *Storia civile del regno di Napoli*. (Indeed, he himself attained this higher plane in the *Triregno*; but that work remained unpublished for more than a century.)

Gallican and Jansenist ideas from abroad were beginning to transform the ecclesiastical-religious environment, reviving indigenous currents of reform. Gallicanism was a political-ecclesiastical movement that leaned toward the national autonomy of the Church while favoring its close association with the state. Jansenism was a dogmatic-ethical movement whose principal elements were an intransigent theory of divine grace and a moral rigor. Gallicanism, based as it was on a certain idea of ancient ecclesiastical organization as opposed to the Roman Curia, managed to climb to the plane of ecclesiastical-religious theory; whereas Jansenism descended from the realm of theory of dogma to attack the ecclesiastical practices and the ecclesiastical policies of governments. Sarpi had already been in close touch with Gallicanism, and had also taken a lively interest in the beginnings of the polemics on grace that later gave birth to Jansenism. In its early phase, Jansenism to be sure was fundamentally a French phenomenon; but it was paralleled by the Italian Augustinians' fight against Molinism and the laxism of the Jesuits.

Jansenism contained much that was antimodern, archaic, and one might even say reactionary. It was based on a rigid conception of dogma revealed and handed down; it moved in the ambit of the old theology with its ancient disputes; and it aimed at the restoration of ascetic morality and ancient ecclesiastical discipline. The principal adversaries of the Jansenists, the Jesuits, were more modern and more accommodating toward the new civilization in various ways. Nevertheless, there were two essential elements of renewal in Jansenism: the first and more important was the restoration of the inwardness of the moral conscience through faith in God's grace, the omnipotent ruler of the elect; the second was the battle against the absolutism of the Roman Church, which gave rise to contacts and then an alliance with Gallicanism. This battle, with its appeal to ancient ecclesiastical traditions, led to a rejuvenation of religious society, and to a prevalence of the Church as a community of consciences over the Church as an ecclesiastical institution and apparatus. Furthermore, there were the continual battles in France against the power of the king, who supported and sometimes even instigated the intervention of Rome. These battles, with their appeal to the superiority of individual conscience over external power, contained within them the seeds of political liberalism, seeds that were to develop in France and Italy toward the end of the century in the climate of the French Revolution.

Objections to the validity and application of the bull *Unigenitus* (1713) and the appeal to a council led to the close association of Jansenism and Gallicanism in France in the first half of the eighteenth century. In this combined form, they were diffused in Italy, joining Italian Augustinianism there and strengthening its innately anti-Jesuitical character. Lombardy, Liguria, Tuscany, Naples, and even Rome (the Bottari circle) participated in the movement; Piedmont did, too, but in a smaller way. In Italy, Gallicanism and Jansenism stimulated the jurisdictional claims of governments, furnishing them with a widened theoretical base and moral impulse. The limitation of the power of the Curia became identified with the independence of governments from the Curia and with the abolition of ecclesiastical privileges. The idea of a national Church became associated with the idea of governmental control and direction of ecclesiastical affairs; both the one and the other nourished hopes and stimulated plans for ecclesiastical reform. Such plans had not only political and social meaning, but religious meaning as well.

In these jurisdictional conflicts and in the anti-Curial battles waged by Italian eighteenth-century governments, a sizable part of ecclesiastical society sided with the sovereigns against the pope. It was probably not the more numerous part, but surely it was the more cultivated and, if we may hazard a guess, it was also the more religious. (In any case, no less religious than the other part.) It was not just the functionaries, the jurists, and the lay writers who preached "royalism"; ecclesiastical canonists, students of patristics and Church history, doctors in theology, and bishops had preached it earlier and better. Royalism was not reducible to simple royal absolutism, and even less to adulation of the sovereign (as Alfieri saw it when he scathingly condemned it in one of his angry polemical outbursts). Royalism included consciousness of the rights of civil society, of the nation, of the people, and of the faithful, a desire for independence from clerical domination, aspirations toward economic and civil progress, concern for the elevation of the people, and, let us repeat it, a tendency toward internal reform, toward the purification and elevation of the Catholic Church to bring Christianity back to its original purity. This religious interest surfaces in Tanucci; it is reaffirmed by the Jansenists in Lombardy; it is realized practically in the work of Scipione de'Ricci, which is then carried on by Peter Leopold. We are not concerned here with evaluating the legitimacy and the results of those movements and those aspirations from a confessional or anticonfessional point of view, but with establishing that they resuscitated the religious problem in Italy, which had been dormant since the time of the Reformation. They reawakened the Italian conscience and stirred its depths, bringing forth the restoration of that moral unity which we saw lost between the Renaissance and the Counter-Reformation; and they contributed substantially to the rise of a new Italy in harmony with the general progress of Europe.

We must, however, establish one essential limitation on both the theory and the practice of the eighteenth-century Italian reform movement with regard to its effect on the Risorgimento: it lacked the participation of the people, and it therefore lacked a broad national base. Italian thinkers of the eighteenth century spoke to a very limited circle, far more limited than was the case in France or England. In Italy, there were no episodes comparable to the agitation of Wilkes in England or to the trials of Calas and La Barre in France (Voltaire!). The people were indifferent or outright hostile to the reform of the governments—witness the devout aversion of the Tuscan people to the reforms of Ricci and Leopold. Moreover, if royalism was not reducible to pure royal absolutism, it is nevertheless true that the strengthening of royal absolutism was its main result, even if not its direct aim. The sovereigns tried through their reforms to improve the administration by making it more uniform, to improve justice by making it more expeditious and more humane, and to improve the economic and intellectual condition of their people by favoring commerce and industry, by abolishing certain levies and impediments to the freedom of work, and by promoting and diffusing culture. But in the end they did not face the fundamental problems explicitly posed by the philosophers, or necessarily derived from their premises—problems which were already very clear to superior minds: civil equality, civil and political liberty, constitutional regulation of the state, and popular control and participation in government. We must therefore simply reject the thesis of Botta and Manzoni, according to which the eighteenth-century Italian reform movement would of itself have led to national resurrection by peaceful and purely indigenous paths if its course had not been interrupted by the French Revolution.

5. The Europeanism of the Italian Eighteenth Century

We must, then, look to the eighteenth century for the beginnings of the Risorgimento; but we must also recognize the clear necessity of looking for the cultural-political conception of the Risorgimento, instead of the political-territorial conception. That is to say, we must climb to a higher level and widen our horizon; we must look at things quite different from the Peace of Utrecht, the Treaty of Aix-la-Chapelle, some piece of territory acquired by Piedmont, or some change in the sovereignty of one or another region of the peninsula. We must—and we insist on this fundamental idea—look at Italy's return to the general course of European civilization and to the general direction of political and social life in Europe.

If we agree on that, the thesis of a purely indigenous Risorgimento will have nothing to gain by the inclusion of the eighteenth century within the Risorgimento. By pushing back its beginnings from the French Revolution to the middle or the beginning of the eighteenth century, the problem of the relationship between the Risorgimento and Europe—i.e., the problem of the foreign influences on the Risorgimento—is moved back in time and in its specific termini; but it returns inevitably, and we have already seen how it is resolved. The political and practical influence of the Revolution is simply replaced by the political and ideological influence of the philosophers.

Research has been done recently on the Italian late eighteenth century (more precisely, on Piedmont) to try to bring to light little-known Italian contributions to letters and science. Although the research has been fruitful in erudite details and praiseworthy for its objectivity, it has not changed the general picture. If anything, it has clouded the picture by failing to distinguish what is important from what is not. An autochthonous Italian eighteenth century, comparable in importance to the predominating currents from abroad, simply has not emerged, and we can swear it never will. As a matter of fact, the idea of an autochthonous life of thought and mind in any country is radically absurd for the eighteenth century, the cosmopolitan century par excellence; even the blind can see that it was a time filled with intense exchanges and reciprocity among the various nations, and that an individualistic-universalistic mentality clearly prevailed. The most important product of the intellectual endeavor of the Italian and European eighteenth century is the concept of humanity, in the double sense of individual development and of a civilization common to all peoples.

Individualism, universalism, humanitarianism, and rationalism are characteristics not only of the Italian eighteenth century but of the French, English, and German as well, though occasionally one of them is emphasized more in Italy than elsewhere. Muratori used to call *ragion di stato* the "fierce disturber of the people's peace," and he exalted those wise princes who knew how to find the true path of glory above all in the welfare of their subjects. Beccaria declared that the criterion of legislation ought to be "the greatest happiness divided among the greatest number." Filangieri asserted that in his time the ancient spirit of aggression no longer dominated; everyone thought only of "living in peace and enriching himself." For Verri, too, the public interest was the sum of private interests. He foresaw a time, perhaps not far off, in which universal reason would expand its dominion; at the same time, he observed that his contemporaries in Europe lived rather similar lives and shared quite similar opinions, and that they could be considered various families within a state rather than diverse nations. He exalted those "noble souls" who "look upon the world as the fatherland of the human spirit, and upon mankind as a family divided into the good and the bad."

This sort of universalism represents a resumption of Italian traditions of both the Renaissance and the Middle Ages, but with a new spirit and a different position with regard to the other nations. At the close of the Middle Ages, Italy attained a position of prominence alongside France (which had formerly dominated), and then passed to a position of outright leadership in the Renaissance. Later came the descent and detachment from the rest of Europe. Now, in the eighteenth century, the Italians understood clearly that they had to climb uphill again, and they looked up to those above them in a spirit of emulation, without envy. In the correspondence of Pietro Verri with his brother Alessandro, he repeatedly refers to Locke, Voltaire, and the Encyclopedists as his teachers. A little later, Verri would associate his memory of Montesquieu with his memory of Beccaria.

All this does not mean that our eighteenth-century writers lacked any sense of nationality. In fact, they occasionally reached a precise formulation of Italian patriotism based on unity and national consciousness. We have just such a formulation in *"Della patria degli italiani,"* published in the *Caffè* and once attributed to Verri, though it was in fact written by Carli. It was only in the minor writers, in those who counted least—the pure scholars, the compilers and editors of historic documents—that national sentiment took on the aspect of hostile rivalry with other countries, attempting (in vain) to affirm an Italian superiority which simply did not exist. It is precisely this weak, sterile, completely ineffectual part of the eighteenth century that some modern scholars like to dwell upon. The more enlightened men of that time felt our inferiority, proclaimed it, and wanted to remedy it not by rejecting foreign progress but by assimilating it.

In the field of political speculation, the absolute prevalence of domestic questions was a counterpart to the universalism and Europeanism of thought in general. We saw that the basic outlines of Italian political thought were the same as those of the rest of Europe. That did not mean that certain problems could not be viewed as particularly Italian, or that certain Italian situations did not require special treatment; it just meant that no one was pretending to do it by creating original principles. The problem of independence was scarcely felt; instead, there was occasionally the problem of getting public opinion to go along with reforms. "Opinion means everything; it directs power," Verri used to say.

The problem of unity was ignored, too; even the idea of a confederation found only occasional and desultory expression. Instead, we see now and then a certain regret for the greatness of the past.

These sentiments sometimes produced judgments and yearnings that were not in perfect accord with the general ideology. Filangieri expounded the idea of public education to form national character; Verri countenanced the hypothesis that a strengthening of the papal system would be beneficial to

Italy, thus establishing a positive connection between the greatness of the papacy and the destiny of the Italian nation. In the conflict between Pope Clement XIV and the Bourbons, he said he felt like a Guelph, adding, however, that it was "because of that natural propensity to side with a courageous underdog." And on the same occasion Baretti (whose ideas were conservative anyway) was outraged that the pope, an Italian prince, should be forced to do the will of foreign powers. He did not stop to reflect that in the question of the Jesuits it was not a matter of the pope as a territorial prince, but as head of the Catholic Church; and that two of the powers attacking him were Italian.

The force and the clarity of sentiment we find in Alfieri are far superior to these vague and occasional hints at patriotic reawakening. Let it be noted that it was only through the fullest recognition of Italian inferiority that he arrived at his famous prophecy of the Revolution and the unity of Italy, which we find in the closing part of his *Del principe e delle lettere*. With this we are actually beyond the eighteenth century, and we can hear the peal of the Risorgimento.

6. *Alfieri and Parini: Moral Revolution*

The peal of the political Risorgimento. We must listen to its sound carefully, so as to make no mistake about the instrument that produced it. It would be a double error to conclude that the political finale we just mentioned and the prophecy of unity in Alfieri's works are grounds for saying he contradicts our conception of the eighteenth century as an ethical-cultural Risorgimento of Europe. Alfieri belongs completely to the second half of the eighteenth century; more specifically, that chapter of *Del principe e delle lettere* was written in 1784, just a few years before the Revolution. Alfieri's relationship to the Italian eighteenth century was similar to that of Rousseau (who was born nearly forty years earlier) to the pure, encyclopedistic eighteenth century: he stands apart from it, and yet carries on its work on the ethical-political plane.

There are moral and cultural—or, more precisely, literary—roots to Alfieri's Italianness. The same is true of his vague nationalism, his pique with other countries, especially France, all of which is something quite different from the spirit that dominated his predecessors. On the one hand, Alfieri recognizes the present inferiority of Italy compared to other countries; he feels his personality affected by it, and is infuriated. On the other, he is overcome by his enthusiasm for the beauty of our literature, and for the harmony of the Italian language (compared to which the sounds of other languages sound almost like bestial screams to his sensitive nerves). He thinks it is impossible to find anyone equal to our four great poets, and he cherishes the hope of occupying a place beside them. The vigorous affirmation of his own individuality is the dominant note in Alfieri; and that alone would render vain and risible any attempt to consider him a champion of statist conceptions, whether for Italy or for society in general. Moreover, that final chapter of *Del principe e delle lettere*, which is generally cited as though it were written separately, stands in fact in close connection to the work as a whole. (Indeed, the connection is much closer than is the case in a more famous final chapter, the one in Machiavelli's *Prince*, to which it bears some resemblance.)

The entire thesis of the work lies in the supreme nobility of the office of writer, so long as it is carried out without any ties to governments and with full freedom of inspiration and expression. Alfieri believes that the destiny of nations is entrusted first and foremost to such writers, for it is they who form and awaken the nation's moral conscience. He expressly and repeatedly maintains the superiority of the great writer to the great prince; likewise, in his *Vita*, he affirms that the dispatches and the diplomacy of the Piedmontese government "seemed to me, and surely were, a far less important or exalted thing than the tragedies that I or others have written." According to Alfieri, it is only when Italian letters will have fulfilled their office—and as a result of that fulfillment—that an Italian political resurrection will become possible. That resurrection will result (most people either don't remember or don't know this) not in unity under a monarch, but in a republic. It is to be foreseen that the single sovereign, who will have replaced the duality (which in turn emerged from the multiplicity) of the Italian states, "will abuse his excessive power, even at home, beyond all limits; but by then the Italians will be united and enlightened; they will have learned to act as a body and to believe in themselves as a single people; and by these united Italians that one and his fateful unity will be abolished, and he will be abhorred and proscribed for many generations."

Alfieri, then, is the most energetic affirmer of the pre-eminence of morality over politics, the champion of the Risorgimento as a spiritual process rather than as a political-territorial fact. Nor could it have been otherwise, for his overcoming (inasmuch as he did overcome) the eighteenth century derives precisely from his emphasis of ethics. Alfieri replaces eighteenth-century utilitarian humanitarianism with moral individualism and with the formation and affirmation of the human personality, which are simply the unfolding and integration of moral individualism. The criticism of Italian education, which was also leveled by other eighteenth-century Italian writers (cf. p. 57), sounds much stronger, much more disdainful in Alfieri. It is the point of departure for his *Vita*, in which he gives the "Second Epoch" the sententious subtitle "Eight Years of Miseducation." In the *Annali*, he writes that he had received from his mother "a very poor education, as is unfortunately customary in Italy." Alfieri continually lashes out against the boarding schools, "non-studies," and pedagogical-disciplinary systems. To his disdain for that sort of education he adds, during the course of his

Vita, two other abominations: military discipline ("the infamous military profession, that damned breed, the soldiery"), and his hatred for the bonds of subjection to the king and for the servility of courts. These two motifs flow together to form an absolute, passionate, angry, and disdainful condemnation of any kind of "tyranny."

All these sentiments spring from Alfieri's fundamental sense of individual freedom and dignity, and then return to that sense. The sentiment is nourished by every experience, and inspires his every judgment, whether it be his judgment of the Prussian military monarchy or the Muscovite despotism, the visit to England at the age of nineteen or the reading of Plutarch (with whom he associates Montaigne and Montesquieu), the prohibition against his leaving Piedmont without royal permission or the prohibition against publishing anything outside Piedmont itself. That was why he was willing to sacrifice his property and his social position, to "de-vassalize" himself: he moved out of Piedmont and cut every feudal bond with his sovereign. Upon leaving Piedmont, he says he could feel himself "breathing easier"; and he goes forth to join the great Lagrange and the lesser Denina as an expatriate. His mind is so made up that any attempt at a "Savoyard" apologia, such as might be tried for the other two men, would be completely pointless; for here we have the uncompromising conscience and will of a man opposed to the environment and the system. His is not a case of personal resentment against his sovereigns, of whom in fact he speaks well; it is rather that "when we think and feel intensely that their usefulness or their harmfulness depends upon their absolute will, we must needs tremble and flee." It is a definitive condemnation of all absolutism, precisely because it is rooted in moral incompatibility. Nor is his position substantially changed by his subsequent opposition to the French Revolution (which he at first had hailed, in his ode *Parigi sbastigliato*). His furious condemnation of France and the Revolution was pronounced in the name of "the sacred and sublime cause of liberty," and against "military arrogance," which lies at the root of the "self-styled republic." He flings in the face of the French, "lowborn slaves," the fact that although France holds Europe in servitude, it is itself held "in a much more bitter and infamous" servitude by a "perpetual consul."

Alfieri, then, moves on a moral plane. A little earlier or contemporaneously, Parini also moved on a moral plane, though the outlook of the two writers was not identical. Despite his Arcadian literary training, Parini had absorbed the social rationalism and utilitarianism of the eighteenth century much more directly and much more broadly than Alfieri. But he, too, affirms the supreme imperative of personal morality (in *L'impostura* and *La caduta*, for examples); he, too, champions individual human dignity against traditional prejudices and social institutions. Although he was not dominated by an urgent need for self-affirmation, as Alfieri was, and although he was much more profoundly influenced by philosophical and Christian humanitarianism, his sense of social justice takes him beyond the boundaries of eighteenth-century political reform, leading him to notions of genuine class conflict (we might even say class hatred) which manifest themselves in the bloody and ironical distichs on the lives of the nobility and plebeians. Even certain moments in the *Giorno* that might be called conservative or nationalistic are in reality manifestations of that fundamental sentiment. He displays it when satirizing the affectation of the nobility in speaking French, when exalting "the Italian Godfrey" above the *Henriade* of Voltaire, and when mocking the extravagance of the nobility in its search of exotic things. It is there when, in speaking of the antireligious tendencies of the "new sophists," he attacks the repugnant class egoism of the nobility, through which it tries to keep the fruits of reason for itself while keeping the people obedient within traditional bonds; and throughout, he uses ironic censure to exalt the social doctrines of equality and humanity in eighteenth-century philosophy. Parini's Christian religiosity is perfectly compatible with his condemnation of the Jesuits and of religious intolerance (his verses against the *auto-da-fé*) and with his opposition to the sort of superstition dominant in Rome.

Parini, like Alfieri, passes from reform to revolution: political revolution for Alfieri, social revolution for Parini. Rousseau had taken the same step; and now the French Revolution was translating it from thought to fact. The French Revolution realized Alfieri's tyrannicidal program too fully, thereby drawing his wrath; but the social sentiments of Parini, when seen in the light of the subsequent Italian revolution, look like a "future" that did not find realization even in the final phase of the Risorgimento. One can say that he was for the Italian revolution at the end of the eighteenth century what Pisacane was for the Risorgimento at its apogee. In any case, it is certain that both Alfieri and Parini fully confirm the ethical-cultural character of the Risorgimento, and its connection with the ideology of the European eighteenth century, of which they represent the final development.

CHAPTER III

The First Revolutionary Crisis

1. From the Reformers to the Jacobins

In the Italian eighteenth century, we have seen a period of harmony between the innovative thought of the writers and the reforming actions of the governments; but of course this harmony was not perfect anywhere, because the thoughts of the writers pushed well ahead of the action of the governments. Moreover, there was an important difference in what inspired them: the governments had not really overcome the principle of *ragion di stato*, whereas the thinkers had decidedly turned their backs on it, assuming instead a concept of the state as the instrument of individual and social well-being. Toward the end of the century, the harmony was completely disrupted: the men in government paused and retreated, whereas the theoreticians moved ahead. The rupture came together with and in relation to the French Revolution; but it had been prepared earlier, for reasons analogous to those that produced the Revolution itself in France.

Two things were lacking in Italian eighteenth-century reform: the participation of the people, which is to say, a truly national consciousness; and the realization of a new, organic ordering of the state—or, in other words, a constitution. These are not lacks that we perceive today with the great advantage of hindsight: Italian thinkers of the time were already cognizant of them. In April, 1796, Verri noted that whatever progress had been made in the preceding years had come about not only by the absolute will of the sovereign, without any impulse from the people, but in fact against the people's feelings, "for they should have liked to preserve the barbarism of torture and the agony of the rack." In 1790, when Leopold II invited the provincial council of Lombardy to put together a list of the complaints and needs of the state, Verri thought that a constitution should be requested, and he wrote a memorandum to that end. Later he wrote a reproach to the Lombard representatives for not having made the request.

Verri took these positions after the French Revolution had begun; but the Revolution probably only prompted him to give expression to conceptions that had matured in him during the preceding decade. We can guess as much from his criticism of Joseph II's revolution from above—criticism, again, written after 1789, but concerned with events that took place earlier. Political progress by royal decree, he writes, is not true progress; it bespeaks absolute government and a police state, "unmasked despotism"; the emperor is no more the master of the people than he is of the public treasury. In any case, Verri's *Decadenza del papato* was written *before* the Revolution, in 1783, though it remained unpublished until after his death. In it, he launches a violent attack against the friars and the "fraud" dominating Italy. He also attacked the system of clerical education, which was based upon blindly and uncritically accepted beliefs, and upon the external observance of rituals and practices without any inner moral life. He attributed the inferiority of the Italians to that kind of education, and called it the cause of the embarrassment that came with saying, anywhere outside Italy, "I am an Italian." Obviously, such education was also made responsible for the indifference and the obscurantism of the popular conscience, and for that lack of national consciousness we mentioned earlier, which sterilized indigenous Italian reform and made it fail.

Many of our writers attacked the friars, among them Parini and Baretti. The spiritual problem of the Risorgimento became the problem of getting the Italian people to attain inner autonomy and a moral life, just as the other European peoples had done. Jansenism had proved inadequate for this purpose—or, at least, had been unable to act in time. It had barely begun to penetrate the universities when the storm of revolution broke out. Parini's *Giorno* and Alfieri's *Vita* are the major manifestations both of the need for moral renewal and of the fact that it had not taken place.

An evolutionary process that is incomplete, but that superior minds still feel the need to complete, is fraught with the seeds of revolution; in the long run, the separation of thought and action, of the ideal and the real, brings about an explosion. The outbreak of the French Revolution caused Italian rulers to stop in their tracks—those rulers, that is, who had moved forward in the first place; but the ideas of forward-looking Italian thinkers were not stopped. They were few, but in those men dwelt the forces of the future. Nothing is more characteristic than the attitude of Verri toward the events of the French Revolution. His was by no means a revolutionary temperament: he was the advocate of a very placid philosophy, and he was a Milanese patrician obedient to the Austrian government, though not always satisfied with it. Nevertheless, he defended the Revolution against those who were scandalized by its initial excesses; he felt sure the movement would spread, and hoped that it would change the face of politics. He accused the privileged classes of not having the impartiality necessary to judge this matter; and although his words were highly critical and even tinged with hatred when the execution of the king and the Reign of Terror took place, he nevertheless did not take a purely negative position toward the Revolution even then. When the Revolution came to Milan, he adapted himself to it, trying to assimilate the new political concepts and forcing himself to understand them according to his rational and moral criteria. He could even look upon revolutionary fanaticism (which went so against his grain) as a possible means for shaking the Italian nation out of its "torpor." If the patrician reformer Verri went that far, others would not sit back and theorize, but would actually try to re-establish the harmony between thought and action. Hence the formation here and there in Italy of Jacobin nuclei, the first conspiracies, the first political trials, and the first death sentences: Emmanuele De Deo, Francesco De Stefanis, Giovan Battista De Rolandis, and others. Filippo Buonarroti, a descendant of Michelangelo, was expelled from Tuscany, and later became a companion of Babeuf in France.

2. *Savoyard Anti-Revolution*

The Italian political-territorial system at the time the French Revolution broke out was not very different (as we have already said) from what it had been three centuries earlier, at the beginning of the foreign invasions: lovely to look at, but not very solid. Innovators in Italy were few; the great majority of the population was composed of faithful subjects, though their faith was for the most part inert and passive. Just as had been the case three centuries earlier, there was as little harmony among the princes as there was solidarity between princes and people. Galeani Napione's much-vaunted plan for confederation (1791) remained nothing but an academic dissertation; indeed, even abstractly considered, it was not a response to a national idea, but rather a way to resist the Revolution, to maintain the status quo: it looked to the past, not to the future. As a matter of fact, it belongs more to the history of the anti-Risorgimento than to the history of the Risorgimento. In any case, the plan was never realized.

Savoyard Piedmont alone pursued an active, warlike policy against the Revolution pressing at the gates of Italy. After almost forty years of French-Austrian accord, which had paralyzed Piedmont's foreign policy, there was a return to the classic position of the House of Savoy, as the balance between the two neighboring great powers. But Victor Amadeus III did not see the situation from this point of view; far from having a national idea, he was not even tempted by the traditional idea of taking Lombardy, which was proposed by revolutionary but still monarchical France in April, 1792. Instead he moved closer to Austria, first to defend, then to recover his possessions on the other side of the mountains, and to block the path of the Revolution. As a matter of fact, moving in a sense completely contrary to the Italian destinies of his house, he even thought of giving the territory of Novara back to Austria, in return for acquisitions in France. Piedmont kept up the battle tenaciously for a few years; but then, under the blows of Bonaparte, it ended precipitously with military disaster, the humiliation of an imposed armistice and peace, French occupation, and finally the expulsion of the dynasty. Except for decrepit Venice, Savoyard Piedmont was more completely wrecked by the first revolutionary crisis of the Risorgimento than any other state. Between 1799 and 1814, the Bourbons played a more active role than the House of Savoy in the anti-Risorgimento reaction (cf. below, p. 61), though Savoy also took part in it before its fifteen-year eclipse.

3. *The First Political Risorgimento*

French arms found the ground in Italy somewhat prepared by the young Jacobins, not only by those who were still alive but by those who had died on the scaffold as well. Side by side with the new generation, which had suddenly become revolutionary, there were reformers who had become Jacobins or who were at least willing to work with them, such as Verri in Milan and Pagano in Naples. The effect on Italian conditions was tremendous. The incipient Risorgimento was transformed from a cultural to a political phenomenon, from governmental reform to democracy, from cosmopolitanism to nationality. The change came as a direct result of the French Revolution, of its ideas, its propaganda, and its victorious campaigns. This is a fact—one of those heavy ones—capable of shattering the sophistical weapons of those advocates of the autochthonous theory. As for the Savoyard theory, it is altogether lost.

When the victorious arms of the republic swept away the old governments—almost without resistance, except for Piedmont —something returned to Italy that had been gone for centuries, since the end of the Middle Ages: political discussion and political struggle, the formation of parties and their conflicts, popular government with representative assemblies—in short, there was a resurrection of national political life. The Italian people returned to the scene and once again became the subjects of history. There was consciousness of this return, of this resurgence; in fact, it was quite clear and even ostentatious, with classical reminiscences abounding in names and institutions. They re-evoked the Italian past, or at least Roman Italy and ancient Rome, thus connecting ideally the two ends of the chain: the very new revolutionary reality and the remote classicism of the republic. Men like Gioia, who were opposed to ancient Rome, reached back even further, to pre-Roman Italy. Even in this classicistic return, the influence of the Revolution was direct and decisive: the Revolution itself had appealed to classical antiquity, to Greco-Roman memories, but above all to Rome, the two Brutuses, Scipio, and Cato.

Classicism was triumphing in arts and letters no less than in political thought. In the latter, it marks the transition from humanitarian cosmopolitanism, which was not devoid of a certain indeterminateness and softness, to a bristling and fanatical patriotic enthusiasm. If there was a radical change in France, which after all had been completely and vigorously conscious of itself as a national state for centuries, the revolution of ideas in Italy, given such a different background, was even greater. The birth of modern patriotism and the beginnings of its transformation into nationalism occurred in France with the French Revolution and in Italy a short time later. Gioia, Cuoco, and Foscolo contemporaneously put forth the idea of "public spirit," or "virtue," by which the citizen feels himself to be completely one with the state; the idea that the fatherland is something to be realized and defended by one's own actions, with arms (Foscolo in particular insists on the necessity for a national militia), with one's entire self; the idea that the safety and life of the nation require a strong, unified state, one which will put all the needs of the national state above everything else. With that, the concept of Italian unity is given a concrete form, as a present need, made urgent by immediate experience. Revolutionary France had triumphed over the coalition thanks to the unified state, its compactness renewed and its energy exalted by Jacobinism. That was why Gioia, in his famous dissertation "Which Form of Free Government is Best Suited to the Happiness of Italy" (1798), fought the idea of establishing many independent republics in Italy, for he knew they would be in disaccord and weak against the foreigner. He even appeals to the negative experience of the age of communes and the age of despots.

All this, of course, did not lead Gioia to abandon the idea of liberty; Italy, he says, owes its regeneration to the revolutionary philosophy that has liberated America and France. (Note the clear sense of the connection between the two revolutions on either side of the Atlantic.) Indeed, one of the main concerns of the dissertation is to show that the Italians have as much capacity for self-government as any other people, both because men everywhere are equal and because there are many proofs of such capacity in Italian history. "It was Italian genius that gave forth the first cry of liberty in Europe" during the Renaissance, and even earlier in the medieval Italian republican movement of the twelfth century, and in fact even in ancient Italy, before the Roman conquest. This last reference is all the more noteworthy for being associated with the re-proach that Gioia, in partial reaction, as we have said, against revolutionary classicism, levels in the most explicit terms against the Roman conquests. "I will not pause to eulogize ancient Rome, nor shall I call its heroes back from the tomb. In fact, I should like to tear the pages of Roman history to shreds, for I see them written with the blood of peoples, and I read there of the enslavement of nations."

This is the first, or nearly the first, link in a chain that will constitute a characteristic line of Risorgimento thought. It reveals the centrality of the liberal concept, and it shows the strong roots of the idea that the new Italianness was to be a product of all segments of the nation, and not a dictatorial imposition by just one part. In another work, Gioia indicated the decisive point in the formation of national consciousness: "Do you all feel you are truly Italian, sons of the same father-land, citizens of the same city? Then you shall be a people, and you may hope for everything. . . . Forget your servile habits, and show yourselves worthy of being governed by free men."

There was a marvelous fecundity in Italian national thought during those three years from 1796 to 1799, thought that was geared toward action and in fact became action. This fecundity alone demonstrates the effect produced by the violent dis-ruption of the old Italy, which the princely reform movement of the eighteenth century had barely scratched. Consider one characteristic point: in that anti-revolutionary plan for an Italian confederation which Galeani Napione devised in 1791, he still found it necessary to discuss over and over again the claims which the Empire still maintained in Italy, and he thought one possibility of confederation might arise from a "solemn renunciation" of those claims. With the violent out-break of revolution in Germany and Italy, those medieval notions of imperial lordship were swept away; the Holy Roman Empire itself collapsed miserably, abdicating after it had been deprived of all authority. Italy was freed of a heavy burden, both real and ideal, that had weighed on her for centuries, a burden which the old Italian states had never been able to throw off.

Once the Risorgimento is understood to be a political-spiritual process, and not a purely political-territorial fact, the positive quality of the revolutionary period stands out clearly and impressively. (Cesare Balbo, on the other hand, relegated the revolutionary as well as the Napoleonic period to the era of foreign domination, which is the equivalent of calling it a new sixteenth century, pure political passivity.) Within three years, all the problems of the Risorgimento were posed: liberty, democracy, independence, federal unification or complete union—in either case under a republican regime. (Union, incidentally, was the solution preferred by the patriots.) The problems were posed in what was at once a concrete, historical, and current form, in relation to the Italian past and present. From Verri to Gioia, from Cuoco to Foscolo, there is a fervor of ideas and discussion. Political journalism and political reviews flourished, especially in Milan, to which people flocked from all parts of Italy. In fact, Milan became the ideal center for the incipient unity of the nation, a unity that found expression even in the songs sung in the streets.

For the first time, unity was being propounded as self-government of the consciously united Italian people. A large and very real step in this direction was taken not only by Venetia and Venice itself, but by Piedmont as well, in the move toward union in the Cisalpine Republic. (In Piedmont, however, there was an Allobroge current that propounded annexation to France. They recalled that the Piedmontese had "once been Gauls," and cursed the Treaty of Cateau-Cambrésis because it had consigned Piedmont to the "tyrant Emmanuel Philibert.") For the first time, the tricolor, the national flag, fluttered in the breeze; and for the first time there were Italian legions, armed bearers of the national idea. Illustrious men entered public life, men capable of incorporating the national idea and of making headway against the French. The religious question was discussed more than ever; there was said to be an intimate relationship between the Gospel and democracy, between Christianity and the freedom of the people. This was the moment when Jansenism freed itself of its royalist fetters and became open liberalism. At the same time, the example of French errors in ecclesiastical politics (the Civil Constitution of the Clergy with its subsequent religious strife) inspired moderation, or, perhaps better, suggested the idea that the religious problem could only be solved in liberty and for liberty, and by means of education.

4. *The Antinomy Within the Italian Jacobin Movement*

Grave consequences were to derive from the fact that the Italian revolution of 1796–99 was brought about by foreign intervention, under the sovereign control of heads of foreign armies, who were the executors of political instructions from a foreign government. The efficacy of the political resurrection was radically diminished, political activity could not proceed normally, political liberties were fettered at the very time they were proclaimed, democracy became largely fictitious and at times was even trampled down. So far as national independence was concerned, it might seem at first blush that it was worse off than it had been before, when only one region of the peninsula was under foreign domination. From this derives the quality of antinomy in this period: on the one hand, it appears to present us with the first political accomplishment of the Risorgimento; on the other, it seems to be a new period of foreign domination (Balbo, above, p. 56). The Italian patriots, or "Jacobins," in the Cisalpine and the Parthenopean republics were among the first to recognize this antinomy clearly. They recognized it because their political program was not an opportunistic improvisation based on the success of French arms, but a conviction that had sprung up in their minds, illuminated by ideas and experience. The men of the Cisalpine and the Parthenopean republics were the same men as or similar in spirit to the ones who earlier had meditated, written, made propaganda, and conspired for the resurgence of Italy. Before the coming of the French, men had died on the scaffold for the new ideas; a few years later, their number was increased by the hundreds felled by Savoyard muskets in Piedmont, or sacrificed on Bourbon gallows in Naples, or transported from Lombardy to Dalmatia by the Austrian government, anticipating the glories of the Spielberg. In this first revolutionary period, Italian patriots realized ahead of time the Mazzinian formula of "thought and action"; their suffering and their sacrifices suffice to give great positive value to the period, despite the shrill laments of nationalistic orthodoxy.

It was not the Italian patriots who put Italy into the position of being buffeted by two overbearing foreign powers. It was not the Jacobins who forced the Republic of Saint Mark into a stupid and vile disarmed neutrality which could only, in those tragic circumstances, lead to ruin. It was not they who told the king of Naples to escape to Sicily, leaving his plebeians to fight alone against the French and to lay violent hands on the best of their fellow citizens. It was not the fault of the Jacobins—even if only for the fact that they were so few—if, at the approach of French troops, the old governments collapsed like houses of cards, and lost everything, starting with honor. Italian independence at the end of the eighteenth century fell with shameful ease because it was no more solid than it had been at the end of the fifteenth century. What was lacking on both occasions was not so much a territorial or legal basis of independence (as Balbo thought), but the backbone of a national consciousness, and the self-creation of the nation by the people.

Both can be found in the ideas and in the works of the Italian Jacobins. They accepted French help because they could not do without it; but they sought to build, to realize Italy by themselves. Civil equality, freedom of thought, renewal of the administrative, political, and social structure were already established; by fortifying the new structures, and by watching carefully for favorable circumstances, they hoped the moment would come when they could rid themselves of their preceptors and make Italy truly free and one. This was not only the secret idea of the Society of the *Raggi*, but the innermost thought, the ultimate spring, of all Italian revolutionary action. Indeed, from the moment the French had arrived, the Italian patriots resisted their influence and insisted upon Italian rights with an energy that may even seem exaggerated to anyone who looks dispassionately at the real situation—which was that the very existence of the Italian republics was based on French arms. Look at the movement of protest (with Gioia and Foscolo in the forefront) against the treaty of alliance, or of vassalage, imposed by the Directory on the Cisalpine Republic; remember, moreover, the furious torrent of indignation over Campo Formio, and before that the many attempts by Venetia and by Venice itself to join the Cisalpine Republic. The idea of Italian unity took on a definite shape precisely as a reaction against the double and contemporaneous experience derived from foreign domination; and in 1799 it was affirmed more solemnly than ever before in official proposals to the French government. Using both idealism and political realism, the Italian patriots tried hard to show France the utility and the necessity of the independence and unity of Italy, according to the European concept of the solidarity and brotherhood of free peoples—a concept that derived from the true revolution, and that anticipated Mazzini and the radical liberalism of Ferrari and Cattaneo.

5. *The First Anti-Risorgimento Outburst*

Because the French were foreign invaders and despoilers, those who rose against them in 1799 and fought for the restoration of old Italy have been pictured as patriots by certain recent publicists. The picture is not accurate. Just to pronounce a few names does not make the thing so. "Not everyone who says to me, 'Oh Lord, Oh Lord,' shall enter the kingdom of heaven." Not all the antiforeign (or perhaps better, "anti-outsider") movements are to be considered national movements. Concern about one's own piece of land, aversion to taxation or conscription, attachment to local customs and even to superstition, the desire to keep one's own property, privileges, and earnings—all these do not justify speaking of a national movement or national sentiment. In fact, it might well mean the direct opposite. It is not enough to speak of independence, or even of aversion to the foreigner: one must see for whom and for what reason independence is sought, for whom and for what reason battle is waged against the foreigner. Independence is not a material-territorial fact, it is a political-spiritual act. Behind it, there must be a people conscious of itself and master of itself. Behind the patriotism of the Sanfedisti, there was only weak, backward, servile Italy, the old Italy that had to disappear before the new could truly rise. Those Neapolitan Lazzaroni, whose valor excited the admiration even of the Jacobins, were fighting for absolutism, religious intolerance, noble and ecclesiastical privilege, and the enslavement of thought. They repudiated the entire positive element of the Revolution.

Moreover, the counter-revolutionaries, or Sanfedisti, of 1799 leaned for support on the foreigner no more and no less than did the Jacobins. It was not Italy, but Austria, fighting with them against France. Both were foreigners; they canceled each other out so far as material independence was concerned. All that remained was the ethical-political difference between the old world and the new. There cannot be even a moment's hesitation in assigning the historical roles: the Jacobins of 1796–99 continued the Italian reform movement of the eighteenth century and represented the Risorgimento; their adversaries represented the anti-Risorgimento. Otherwise we should have to consider Fra Diavolo and Brandaluccioni as precursors of Garibaldi—which would be logical enough for those who want to expel Mazzini ("the republican leprosy") from the Italian Risorgimento. We must add, too, that if the victims of the Bourbon reaction are commonly and rightly considered to be precursors of the Risorgimento, the same is true of the victims of the monarchial reaction in Piedmont in 1797–98, before the expulsion of the dynasty, even though the events in Piedmont were not on the same level with events in Naples, and even if the Bourbon reaction was far more atrocious, far more disdainful of justice and humanity. It is through those victims that Piedmont really begins to take part in the Risorgimento.

6. *Napoleonic Reaction*

Compared to the revolutionary period, the Napoleonic period represents a definite regression, which was a direct reflection of the whole Napoleonic mentality and the politics of the Empire.

Even now, there are some differences of interpretation regarding Napoleon's position toward Italy, both with regard to his national consciousness as a man and to his concrete Italian policies as a ruler. Nevertheless, two things are clear: Napoleon Bonaparte considered himself French, and he thoroughly and completely subordinated the interests of Italy to those of France. His instructions to the Viceroy Eugene spoke clearly on this point, even before his actions did. The most that can be said is that at the time of the Directory, Napoleon showed a very specific interest in Italy, because he considered it a base for his fortunes, a reserve, or a launching point. And so he played a role in arousing the people of the Po Valley, and promoting the Cispadane and Cisalpine republics; but this was more than offset both by his absolutism toward the new republic, and by his commercial handling of Campo Formio, hateful in itself, but even more on account of the scorn and trickery with which he saw fit to accompany it.

Once Napoleon had finally accomplished his leap into the government and the throne of France, his specific and predominant interest in Italy disappeared. One might say that the positive qualities in Napoleon's policies toward Italy derive from the Revolution, whereas the negative are all his own. Or, to formulate it more broadly, one might say that in Italy as elsewhere Napoleon acted like a great natural phenomenon that upsets and transforms the environment with its violent action and, without wanting or knowing it, opens the way for forces it did not create.

The beginnings of political autonomy were truncated by Napoleon in Italy as they were in France. The constitution of the Kingdom of Italy quickly became a parody; we need only recall what happened to the legislative body when it permitted itself to propose modifications in the draft of a law sent from Paris. Although it gave in immediately, the legislative body was suppressed, just as freedom of the press was suppressed in fact, though it existed legally. All this brought about stagnation; after the fervor and the splendor of the end of the century, culture declined. Before long, shadows of gloom fell over Napoleonic Italy. The depression also had its effects on national thought: Cuoco and Gioia resigned themselves to justifying the absolutism of Napoleon with opportunistic arguments—among them, the need for protection, and the need for a strong central government for a people with great interests to protect, a people in grave danger.

This practical resignation, masked with arguments, is accompanied by a genuine involution of ideas. Cuoco winds up with a fatalism that extinguishes all energy, with a mathematical balance of good and evil in perpetual equilibrium. The force that animates nature is unique and eternal; men change, but humanity is always the same, and cannot resist the superior order that drags it along; an equal sum of virtue and truth is always balanced by an equal sum of vice and error. Foscolo, with a realism crude to the point of ingenuity, enthrones the concept of a dominating force which, fusing with the naturalism and materialism left over from the eighteenth century, takes on a universal and cosmic value, and also ends in a fatalistic and pessimistic conception. The whole of mankind cannot live in peace or freedom; men must be subjected to the minds of the wise or the dominion of the strong. That is why the human race is divided into many servants and few masters. He mocks "the sublime contemplations" which confuse "factual truth with metaphysical vision," and proclaims in precociously Hegelian language: "Everything that is must be; if it should not have been, it would not have been." There is no natural equity: the rights of peoples are resolved by force, and the state of war among peoples is fundamentally perpetual. Foscolo sees the national state as the only remedy for the "war of all against all." He concludes that "justice exists in particular societies, but not in the universal society of the human race," and that justice resides within the terms of *ragion di stato*. And so, almost as soon as it was born, the idea of nationality fell into nationalism and statism. At the end of the Napoleonic period, in the discourse *Of the Servitude of Italy* (1815), Foscolo envisages a monarchy in which the nobility holds the balance between the king and the citizens, while the masses are excluded from all political office, and even, one might say, from the society of the nation. This last may well have been the result of experiences with the Sanfedisti at the end of the preceding century, and even more of the slaughter of Prina in Milan, when the Kingdom of Italy fell.

7. The Equivocal "Kingdom of Italy"

From the point of view of the Risorgimento, the greatest positive element in the Napoleonic period seems to be the Kingdom of Italy, because of its vastness, its organization, and its very name. We would be deceived, however, if we thought that Napoleon intended to create an Italian kingdom that was compact and well-defended. After Marengo, the First Consul had ordered a program of military construction that enhanced the defenses of France and diminished those of Italy. Still more significant is the fact that Piedmont and Liguria were annexed to France, so that the gates to Italy on that side were not only ajar but wide open. Napoleon was so insistent on this point that even in March, 1814, when he was forced to allow Eugene and Murat to divide Italy between them if they could, he made exception of those two regions, which he did not intend to renounce. From Liguria, the Napoleonic Empire was trying to drive a wedge into the Kingdom of Italy between Lombardy and Emilia, by occupying and then annexing the Duchy of Parma and Piacenza. The wedge was reinforced by the Grand Duchy of Tuscany, a fief of the Empire, under Elisa Bonaparte Baciocchi. The Kingdom of Italy got the Marches, taken from the pope, but not Umbria, which was joined to the Empire together with Rome and Latium. And so the Kingdom of Italy, excluded from the Tyrrhenian Sea, looked very curious: a quadrilateral, irregular on the north, with a long tail between the Apennines and the Adriatic, up to the Neapolitan border. This completely arbitrary configuration and delimitation should be enough to show that Napoleon considered the Kingdom of Italy an expedient, not a goal.

Soon after 18 Brumaire, Francesco Melzi d'Eril (who later became a good vice-president of the Italian republic—but not viceroy of the kingdom, because by then Napoleon was only placing members of his family) wrote to Napoleon lamenting that the renewal of Italy was not being accomplished with a precise program. "There was only one [program] and it was great, the only great one: to join all the peoples and re-create a nation. But the grandeur of the result aroused fear!" Naturally, Napoleon had his usual argument ready in such cases: Italy was not mature. A more fitting explanation would be to repeat that Napoleon was the sovereign of France, and that he always looked at the affairs of Italy from the French point of view (taken in the traditional sense of the old politics). He once wrote to the Viceroy Eugene, apropos of some question of customs tariffs: "Italy must not contemplate anything that would detract from the prosperity of France; she must fuse her own interests with those of France. Above all, she must be careful not to give France an excuse for an-nexation, for if France found it to be in her interest, who could stop her?" In reality, politically speaking, annexation was already an accomplished fact.

Still, it would be a mistake to conclude that as a result of Napoleonic despotic rule there was only passive obedience in the Kingdom of Italy. There was the great fact that the administration of this kingdom, which was the largest state Northern Italy had seen for many centuries, was almost entirely in the hands of Italians. Neither was it an inactive administration, or one that limited itself to conservative mea-sures. Set in motion by Napoleon, the administration went to work with great intensity; so far as civil relationships and economic conditions were concerned, they may be said to have accomplished through revolution what the Italian reforms of the eighteenth century had begun. Feudal and economic fetters disappeared, as did mortmain, privileges of pri-mogeniture, special legislation, and special tribunals; there came civil equality, administrative regularity and centraliza-tion, and unity of weights and measures. Furthermore, there came measures for public education and hygiene, encourage-ment of industry and commerce through the disappearance of customs barriers and tolls, a grandiose development of the network of roads and of public works, an enlargement of cities, and progress in industry and agriculture.

The creation of an army in the Kingdom of Italy was of no small importance. That, too, had not been seen for centuries. To be sure, foreigners created it and held the supreme command, and it almost always fought for foreign interests (who can forget the verses of Leopardi on the Italians who fell in Russia?); but the cadres, including the generals, were Italian, as were the troops. The army provided technical training, a school for energies, a hotbed (whether Napoleon liked it or not) for national sentiment, a crucible for creating unitary feeling. It was no accident that in the first years of the Restoration the former officers of that army were in the front line among the agitators and conspirators for Italian independence and liberty. Even in 1848, survivors of the army worked for the national cause.

8. *The Ambiguity of Napoleon*

In conclusion, Napoleon presents a double face for Italy, as he does for France and the rest of Europe. He had made a selection in the revolutionary inheritance of the eighteenth century, based on his temperament and on his personal vicissitudes, accepting a part (equality, economic and technical growth) and rejecting the rest. But such selections are made by history, and not by the will of any single individual, no matter how great. Napoleon never succeeded in getting rid of the revolutionary principle of popular will; in fact, he was forced to build his own edifice (plebiscites) formally upon it, though he saw to it that it functioned as he wished. Even as he was unsuccessful in extinguishing individual opposition, explicit or tacit, he saw the national-liberal demands of the peoples rising about him, and at Saint Helena he recognized that he had made a mistake. But then, even Napoleonic equality had some very strange characteristics: with the re-establishment of a court that imitated the pomp of Versailles under Louis XIV, with the institution of an imperial nobility, including principalities furnished with territorial appanages, and with the multiplication of vassal kingdoms, one might well speak of a new feudalism.

This substantial ambiguity in Napoleon gave rise to a great confusion of ideas and sentiments in the Italian political world and elsewhere. The reaction against Napoleonic despotism was just as ambiguous as Napoleon himself, for it attacked the progressive aspects of Napoleon's work no less than the reactionary. In the Napoleonic period, counter-revolution could disguise itself as patriotism much more easily than in the republican period. The confusion reached such a point that when the Kingdom of Italy fell, the pro-Austrian party could seem to be representing Italian independence. (We must remember that the anti-Napoleonic allies spoke of independence and freedom of the peoples.) The ambiguity was also responsible for the failure to maintain—or, rather, to establish—a truly independent Italian kingdom, or at least one that was seriously autonomous. The moral roots of Austrian dominion in Italy were set by Napoleon; at the beginning and at the end of his career, he found he had worked for that dominion.

This confusion in the purely political sphere was accompanied by confusion in the realm of religious politics, heightened by the conflict between Napoleon and Pius VII, who morally restored the papacy. Hints of neo-Guelphism and neo-Ghibellinism intertwined, for example, in the thought of Foscolo; on the one hand, he recalled the arguments of Gregory VII, and spoke of educating the Italians to arms and to the liberty the popes had brought about; on the other, he recalled the papal appeals for foreign intervention, and reproved Napoleon for not having let the papacy "live on charity and languish in consumption." This confusion played no small role in rendering the Italian people passive witnesses to the great events of 1814–15, and in particular to Murat's attempt at unity.

9. Austrian Restoration

The political and territorial arrangement of Italy in 1815 is strikingly similar to the arrangement of 1784, which is natural enough since there was a "Restoration." Nevertheless, there is one significant difference, and that is the increased power of Austria, which is now clearly predominant throughout the entire peninsula. Having recovered Lombardy and at the same time reacquired Venetia (which in 1797 it had only received in exchange for Lombardy), Austria was mistress of Northern Italy. Moreover, she now had the powerful support of the entire contiguous Empire, whereas in the eighteenth century Lombardy was close but detached. Added to this strengthened position was a more decided will to control and command, a will that manifested itself in the treaties with Tuscany and Naples, the latter giving Austria the right to interfere in its internal affairs. It also manifested itself in the principle of intervention, which Austria made the other great powers accept. They, on the whole, were satisfied to consider Italian affairs as matters of Austrian interest and competence. It was a high imperial sovereignty, re-established in a far more concrete and efficient form than the earlier one.

France could no longer act as a counterbalance to Austrian power (at least not to the extent it had done earlier) because it was a defeated state, at the margin of great politics, and controlled by an anti-Napoleonic alliance that continued under the name of the Holy Alliance. Spanish influence in Southern Italy, already diminished in the time of Marie Caroline to make way for Austrian influence, now ceased altogether, just as the position of Spain itself as a great power had disappeared. Instead, Russia, which represented a new counter-balance to Austria, now extended its rivalry from Germany and the East to Italy. In fact, Russia had already come to Italy at the end of the preceding century, through the wars of the anti-French coalition. At that time, the czars had protected the Kingdom of Piedmont against the appetite of Austria, and they did the same during the Restoration. England was in sympathy with the protection of Piedmont; but because of her Mediterranean interests England looked more toward the South, and especially toward Sicily, where an English procon-sul had succeeded in temporarily imposing the constitution of 1812 upon the Bourbons (who were suspect to Eng-land because of their family ties to France and Spain). On the whole, except for Austria, the other powers had only limited and secondary interests in Italian affairs. No one was able or disposed to contest Austrian supremacy; there was nothing resembling the former equilibrium between France and the Hapsburgs, upon which the House of Savoy had been able to base its policies up to 1748. Italian patriots (like Foscolo) now began to discuss the idea that an Italy restructured into a na-tion would be useful for the equilibrium and peace of Europe (a variation on the idea of the Italian republicans of 1799, who spoke of the association of free peoples); but their words found no audible echo in the chancelleries of Europe.

10. *Piedmontese* Ancien Régime

With no foreign efforts being made in favor of Italian inde-pendence, there remained the abstract possibility of an under-standing among the Italian states to form a counterbalance to Austria. But it was precisely a purely abstract possibility. The Italian governments of the Restoration knew full well that they formed part of a system with its base in Austria, and that an anti-Austrian coalition would have meant taking on Europe of the Congress. Moreover, two of the princes of Italy were

Austrians, and the largest Italian state, Naples, was tied to Austria by a treaty. Austria feared an Italian confederation so little that she herself proposed one, though unsuccessfully, so that she could become head of it.

Piedmont was against the alliance and the confederation, though its opposition did not derive from a sense of Italian national policy. That is also true of the rather active territorial policy pursued by Victor Emmanuel I at the time of the Restoration. That policy was intended to preserve his own dominion on either side of the Alps (Savoy, Novara), and to extend it to Genoa and Lombardy. This latter objective, the greatest of all, was the only one that might have taken on a national character; but it failed. Victor Emmanuel I and his ministers did not make a direct appeal to the new national forces; instead, they merely pointed them out in the background to the great powers, in order to regain the role of counterbalance, this time between Russia and Austria, and between England and France; and they, too, had recourse to the concept of equilibrium. The absorption of Genoa realized an ancient objective of Savoyard politics, but not without arousing resistance, regrets, and aversion among the Genoese. If, above and beyond Piedmontese territorial expansion, the absorption of Genoa brought positive national consequences (such as the infusion of freer spirits into Savoy, Jansenist currents, social elements different from the closed and old-fashioned Piedmontese-Savoyard aristocracy), they were indirect consequences, certainly not intended by those who governed in Turin.

Substantially, Piedmont and Naples were on the same level with regard to Italian politics in general. If Piedmont felt the problem of independence from Austria more strongly, Naples had on its side the traditions of Murat as a ferment for change. In particular, it had the army of Murat, which, though fused with the legitimist army, still kept the old leaders. Another specific element of subversion in the South was the Sicilian autonomist and separatist movement. However, it had a strictly local character, without repercussions on the continent; it was founded not so much on a new will to self-determination as it was on legal appeals to the past (though in truth partly to a very recent past, the constitution of 1812). The other Italian states had no importance in general Italian politics.

11. *Restoration and Anti-Risorgimento*

The question has been raised whether the domestic policies of the European states after 1815 may properly be called reactionary; or, to put it another way, whether there was a pure and simple restoration of the pre-Revolutionary past, of the *ancien régime*. Everyone now agrees that the sovereigns at the Congress of Vienna did not intend to carry out any such complete restoration. They, too, wanted to choose, to make a synthesis between old and new, and they wanted to do it according to Napoleonic principles, though partly attenuated. Like Napoleon, though far more decidedly, they returned to the old order; their innovation was the principle of legitimacy, which Napoleon for obvious reasons had not been able to invoke (and he could never get over it). But they used the principle of legitimacy the way he had used the principle of popular sovereignty. Both Napoleon and the legitimist princes wanted, after all, to continue the enlightened absolutism practiced by eighteenth-century sovereigns; and both failed to recognize how anachronistic it was.

Enlightened absolutism had represented a partial application of ideas and explication of forces that later found their ultimate historical outlet in the Revolution. One could hardly, therefore, go back to enlightened despotism, which would have meant forcing back to its modest source a river that had already flowed broadly through the plain. What had been historical progress under eighteenth-century enlightened absolutism became, under Napoleon and his antagonist-continuers of 1815, antihistorical reaction, devoid of moral force because not based on coherent principles. The Prince of Canosa and Monaldo Leopardi were right in their criticism of the Restoration.

So far as Italy is concerned, the problem takes this specific form: whether the Restoration and the Risorgimento are antithetical, or whether the work of the restored governments is not to be included at least partially in the process of the Risorgimento. In other words, was the Risorgimento a revolution against the Restoration, or did it evolve out of it? In general, those who opt for the latter, which means those who try to turn the Restoration to account through the Risorgimento, are the same ones who lend credence to the political-territorial interpretation of the Risorgimento itself. But, as a matter of fact, it is precisely from this political-territorial point of view that the Risorgimento appears to be revolutionary. What else can we call a process by which seven governments are reduced to one through the conquest of the other six? On political-institutional and ideological grounds, too, there can be only one answer; and we already gave it earlier when we spoke of the anachronistic character of the "enlightened" absolutism of the restorers. Although the men of the Congress of Vienna accepted certain political-social changes, and even some constitutional institutions (in a few cases outside of Italy), they did not countenance the ideas of nationality and liberty, which implied the right of peoples and of individuals to determine their own destinies. They held that only the king was entitled to provide for the well-being of his subjects, and that there was to be no interference from or responsibility to the people or individuals. Those who governed received their power directly and only from God. The fundamental principles of the Restoration and those of the Risorgimento were, then, antithetical. Whether the latter triumphed fully—whether, that is, the political-ideological revolution was as completely successful as the political-territorial revolution—is a matter which we shall try to determine later.

Italy of the Restoration represented a substantial regression not only when compared with the earlier Italy of the Revolution, but even when compared with Napoleonic Italy, which was already a reaction. We saw how Napoleon, with all his despotism (and in part thanks to it), had stirred up the old world, had brought new forces and new classes to the field of public action, and maintained (despite his innermost tendencies) the principles of popular sovereignty in place of the ancient principle of divine right. The requirements of empire forced him to try to still the excitement of the new life, but at the same time to heighten it. All this disappeared with the Restoration. In fact, Italy of the Restoration appears to be reactionary even when compared with the pre-Revolutionary Italy of eighteenth-century reform. The individual achievements of the reform movement were maintained in some cases; but the orientation, the spirit, changed. What had once been a push forward became an arresting blow; the point of departure became the point of arrival, the impassable Pillars of Hercules. Whenever the achievements of eighteenth-century reform or of the Revolutionary-Napoleonic period were maintained, they were maintained for fear of upheavals and inasmuch as they were the instruments of absolutism: which is to say, they were maintained in a conservative-reactionary spirit. "Of all things restored, the only one overlooked was the restoration of the reforming and progressive spirit of the eighteenth century" (Balbo).

The change is particularly clear in ecclesiastical policy. Because the principle of divine right of princes had been shaken by the ideas and events of the Revolution, the governments of the Restoration found it necessary to turn to the Church to have it strengthened, and so they favored and exalted the Church before the people. This brought about a marked reaction against the religious liberalism and laicism of the eigh-

teenth century, the abandonment of any pretense at ecclesiastical reform, and the end of all governmental anticlericalism.
Another result of the change was that many of the Italian
and non-Italian governments entered into negotiations with
the Holy See, leading to concordats or similar agreements, to
settle the ecclesiastical situation in the various countries and to
heal as much as possible the breach between the two powers.
It was, in sum, a clear return to the alliance between throne
and altar, with the latter getting the greater prestige not only
because of its resistance to Napoleon, but also because of the
new intellectual attitudes (romanticism, medievalism) quite
independent of governmental orientations.

An episode that characterized this political-religious change
was the re-establishment of the Jesuit Order, carried out by
Pius VII in 1814. There was not a single protest from any
government, Bourbon or non-Bourbon, Italian or non-Italian,
though some of them did indeed maintain the eighteenth-
century decrees against the Order for a short time. The Jesuit
Order was soon as widespread and influential as ever, adding
to its ancient devotion to the papacy a strenuous attack on
liberal ideas. For a while, Austria and Tuscany preserved a
large part of the tradition of Joseph and Leopold; but even so,
the spirit had changed, in the direction of pure jurisdictional-
ism; no longer was the hope harbored of overcoming ecclesi-
asticism and moving toward a new civil and religious society.
Events moved in a direction favorable to the Church, culminating in the Tuscan concordat of 1851 and the Austrian concordat of 1855. Nevertheless, on the whole those two states
kept themselves on a higher plane than the other Italian states.
The Papal States with Cardinal Consalvi attempted something
resembling eighteenth-century reform; Naples preserved substantially the inheritance of Murat; and Savoyard Piedmont
was the most "Restorationist," that is to say, the most
reactionary.

CHAPTER IV

The Definite Formulation

1. The Liberalism of the Carbonari

The main difference between the eighteenth century and the period of the Restoration is that in the former there was agreement between the government (at least in some cases) and progressive public opinion, whereas in the latter there was profound disagreement, a dissidence pregnant with revolutionary possibilities. Progressive circles in Italy were completely disappointed by the new arrangement, and the subsequent behavior of governments only served to deepen the disappointment. And so it came about that reform by princes was succeeded by revolution by the people—if not by the whole people, at least by the most enlightened and active part. No matter what the character of their demands—that is to say, even when they were temperate and modest—the very request assumed revolutionary proportions in the face of the negative attitude of the governments.

Of the various problems posed before the Italian political consciousness in the revolutionary years at the end of the eighteenth century, the problem of unity was the one that seemed least pressing during the first years of the Restoration. True, in 1815 Manzoni was already affirming that "we shall never be free if we are not one"; and later, in 1821, he was insisting on the fundamental idea of the unity of Italy, "One in arms, language, altar, memories, blood, and heart"; but the conspirators between 1815 and 1830 used the idea of unity more as a general longing for association or unification rather than as a program for a unified state embracing all of Italy.

Essentially, what they wanted was liberty and a constitution, demands derived from the Revolution, and reinforced by the revolt against the tyranny of Napoleon and of his continuers. The Carbonari became the interpreters of this liberal mood. Born in the South in opposition to Murat, who refused to grant a constitution, the movement was allied for a while and to an extent with the Bourbons. But later, because of the disappointment we mentioned, it quite logically became anti-Bourbon; and later still, it began to spread throughout the peninsula. The importance of the Carbonarist movement consists precisely in its having propagated liberal-constitutional demands, with unity of aspirations, in all of Italy and, in fact, throughout Europe.

Carbonarism flourished in France no less than in Italy, and the bonds between the movements in the two countries were very strong. One of the chief elements of the new times (an element produced by the French Revolution and one which the Restoration could not suppress, but rather nourished) was the formation of a common European public opinion and state of mind that transcended the borders of the individual states, so that any movement of ideas or any event in one state had immediate effects and repercussions in the others. In this connection, we must recall one fact that is given scant attention by the general historical consciousness of today, a fact that at first seems somewhat strange: it is that Napoleon, dethroned and exiled by the Holy Alliance, was transformed into a symbol of liberty in France, in Italy, and in the rest of Europe. This transformation is connected with another fact; namely, that the armies were hotbeds of the liberal movement. For these reasons, revolutionary uprisings were not considered isolated occurrences within an individual country, but rather took on the aspect of European crises.

The fundamental idea of this liberal-Carbonarist European public opinion was that individual liberty and national liberty (or independence) had to be considered together as a harmonious pair. The individual's freedom to develop was considered the incontestable right of each man, just as the free development of its own nationality was the ineradicable right of each people. The rights of individuals were of the same nature as the rights of nations; and the latter, in good eighteenth-century fashion, were considered to be the sum of the former. A people had its rights inasmuch as it consisted of human beings; the rights of the nation did not transcend individual rights, but were the sum or the result of them.

The weaknesses of the Carbonarist movement were the vagueness of its political program (which in fact is little known even today); and a certain tendency to compromise with governments—a tendency so strong that the Carbonari even considered supporting an antiliberal government now and then (Metternich's Austria, France under Charles X). The fact of this weakness was accompanied by another fact, perhaps of identical origin: namely, that in the period 1815–30, Italian political thought, so remarkably developed from the middle of the eighteenth to the early years of the nineteenth century, remained arrested in the Napoleonic phase. Aside from Romagnosi's individualistic positivism and legal constitutionalism (a rather impoverished continuation of eighteenth-century thought), we find a current or, rather, several currents which can be called "antipolitical," not in the sense that term had in the police jargon of the time (i.e., a subversive tendency against the constituted order), but in the sense that they arrived at a pessimistic disesteem for the value of human activity through the denial or debasement of political values in general. Nevertheless, the disesteem contained certain elements that had a notable effect on the intellectual course of the Risorgimento: the radical negation of *ragion di stato*, which was being used once again by the governments and by conformist thinkers; the clear subordination of political interests to moral needs; and the affirmation of the purely instrumental value of governments and states with regard to humanity. We find such sentiments expressed both by the Christian Manzoni and by the unbeliever Leopardi.

2. *Lombard Reform and the* Conciliatore

The tendencies toward political compromise in the Carbonarist movement were not discordant with the social-economic reform movement that gained ground in the first years of the Restoration, especially in Lombardy. The movement appears to be very much a continuation of the eighteenth century, except that there is much more shunting from theory to practice. And since it used private rather than governmental energies, it seemed to have the character of popular-national initiative. The accomplishments of Confalonieri, Porro, and the others of their group included the introduction of the steamboat, the spinning jenny, and other things. They promoted elementary education, and then nursery schools; they sided with the Romantic movement in literature against the Classicists supported by Austria, who "defended grammar, the principle of authority, and the papacy"; and they founded the *Conciliatore*.

The social-cultural reform movement, which continued in Lombardy until 1848, played a considerable role in the elaboration of Risorgimento forces. The writers of the *Conciliatore* are the successors of such eighteenth-century Italians as Verri and Beccaria, whom they exalted as the "heroes of reason." They declared that they were striving to promote the general welfare, guided by reason and experience. Their criteria of judgment and their objectives of action were always in keeping with progressive reform, the inheritance of the preceding century. And, like the reform movement, the *Conciliatore* and the entire current associated with it were outspoken Europeanists; for them the problem of rejoining Italy to Europe was very acute. Di Breme wrote in the *Conciliatore*: "As everyone knows, Italy is still sleeping in Aristotle's thought, and meanwhile European thought is progressing. . . . At large in the world are many ideas, many concepts, many perceptions, to which the Italians have not yet given form; there are no words and no forms in our dictionary for morality, economics, metaphysics, domestic life. . . . It is far less urgent for us to speak the way Cardinal Bembo did, and as certain bigwigs in the holy Crusca do, than it is to participate fully in the benefits of human culture and intellectual civilization. . . ." These last words were directed against the purism of the Abbé Cesari and others. If they are a bit unjust, they are nevertheless useful as a counterbalance to the occasional and excessive exaltation of purism as a fundamental contribution to the Italian national consciousness.

Austria could have tried to make use of the reform movement, especially since Italian liberal-progressive opinion and even the Carbonarist movement were ready to recognize the civil superiority of the Austrian government to the other governments in the peninsula. Indeed, there were even some vague notions of extending its dominion to other regions of Italy, particularly to the Legations. Instead, Austria immediately joined battle with the reform movement; and the *Conciliatore*, despite its literary quality, was suppressed after only one year of life. This was the beginning of a reactionary rigidity, a paralysis of brain and will that served to distinguish the Austrian ruling class almost uninterruptedly for a century, up to the catastrophic end of the Hapsburg Empire. The Austrian government came to be considered foreign and oppressive by the Italian national consciousness—something which had not happened in the eighteenth century. Furthermore, Austrian preponderance in all of Italy gave clearer outline to the problem of unity by tying it to the problem of independence. From this time on, the new political orientation gained ground, with conspiracies and the first insurrectional uprisings. Since legal action was rebuffed, it was necessary to turn to illegal action. Italy was not the "land of the dead." That goes not only for Austrian Lombardy and Venetia but for all of Italy.

3. *The Uprisings of 1820–21*

The uprisings of 1820 and 1821 (the revolutions in Naples and Piedmont) represented the first genuine revolutionary initiative of the Risorgimento, for the upheavals at the end of the eighteenth century had taken place as a result and with the help of French intervention. The importance of these uprisings lies not only in the fact that they represented an initiative, but also in the fact of their international ramifications. The years 1820–21 constitute a primary episode in the history of European Carbonarism. The upheaval began in Spain, spread to Italy, and made itself felt even in France; then it circled back and ended where it had begun, in Spain, under the blows of the French-Bourbon army that came to re-establish absolutism. (The Italian absolutist reaction was represented by Charles Albert of Carignano, hereditary prince of Sardinia.) Italian national sentiments and Europeanism were closely associated in those upheavals; the Italian Risorgimento was conceived of and tried out as an element in a new Europe. The Italian problem was now posed as a European question before the governments of the great powers, who had more or less ignored its existence at the Congress of Vienna. It caused the first split among the conservative Quintuple Alliance: the views of France and England differed from those of the Holy Alliance of the three northern powers; but they nevertheless remained passive in the face of Austrian action. A little later, events in Latin America and Greece caused the final detachment of England from the conservative bloc, and the temporary and partial detachment of France and Russia.

Although the Italian upheavals of 1820–21 were broadly European on the political-geographical level, they were very restricted on the political-social level. In Italy, as in Spain and France, it was essentially the army that had taken part in them; that is to say, we are dealing with "pronunciamentos." But we must recall that the character of the armies had changed in the preceding period: in France, the defense and the revolutionary conquest had brought about the change; in Spain, it came through the war of independence; and in Italy through the formation of the army of the Republic and then of the Kingdom of Italy. The armies had entered into a close relationship with the new revolutionary-national order, and had been tested in battle against the old Europe. The army was no longer the royal-governmental mercenary instrument of the *ancien régime:* it came forth as the representative of the nation, the bearer of the national idea, above and beyond— and, when necessary, against—kings and governments. It had its own ethical-political consciousness, which was capable of breaking the chains of professional discipline in the name of a higher imperative. But the army played the role of protagonist in the Risorgimento for only a fleeting moment. (In Spain, the army degenerated to the dismal point of actually issuing pronunciamentos, of a factious and personal kind.) After having succumbed very easily before foreign arms, the army in Naples and Piedmont reorganized itself quickly within state-dynastic limits. That had its advantages and disadvantages, which it is not our job to describe.

What remains, then, is that the upheavals of 1820–21 had a certain quality of caste (together with a trace of particularistic interests), and a very restricted social base. Not only did the people play no real role in the movement, but neither did the middle classes: the insurrectionists were for the most part

officers and noblemen. The Carbonarist movement had penetrated the army, but had not renewed the conscience of the
country. A sect went into action while the people remained on
the sidelines; and so far as the pronunciamentos were concerned, they were felt to be something of an imposition on the
country. Even within the very restricted segment of activists,
there were discernible uncertainties, contrasts, and imperfections in their ideas. In Naples, the residual Muratism, which
played a principal role in the new government, was different
from and hostile to Carbonarism. The Neapolitan movement
gave no sign of striving for unity, while Sicily reaffirmed its
separatism; the insurrectional junta at Alessandria spoke of
Italian federation and of a kingdom of Italy; but they meant a
kingdom of Northern Italy. Manzoni's call to unity (see above,
pp. 75–6) never got beyond the poet's study. Still, the tricolor,
already the symbol of national unity, waved again; and the almost contemporaneous national-revolutionary upheaval in
North and South in a way anticipated—inversely—the situation of 1860. But in both places the insurrectionists meant to
preserve their respective dynasties, and that in itself precluded
a unitary development. The Carbonari at Naples would accept
the Bourbons, provided they gave a constitution; and the
Carbonari in Turin were not only faithful to the Savoyard
dynasty, but in their program for a constitutional kingdom of
Northern Italy they went so far as to associate the aggrandizement of the dynasty with the national cause. Santarosa and
his friends were taking up the traditional Savoyard program,
sublimating it in the light of the nation and liberty: the dynas-
tic-territorial interest was being raised to an ethical-political
postulate.

In Naples, the dynasty accepted the revolution and then
reneged, therewith beginning its policy of perjury. In Turin,
the dynasty did not accept the offer of elevation, not so much
because of the risk involved as because it was still tied to
ancien-régime ways of thought. It expected aggrandizement

through conquests, treaties, and traditional law, not through a national-revolutionary will. Men who had asked the czar for Lombardy did not intend to receive it from Santarosa and Confalonieri. To preserve the absolutism of divine right, they preferred the territorial status quo and the renunciation of aggrandizement; that was why they called for Austrian arms against men who were devoted to them and desired their greatness. The Savoyard monarchy was not only a stranger, but hostile to the Risorgimento. Though their tone was very different, Victor Emmanuel I and Charles Felix were both very logical and honest, and acted without hesitation. The same cannot quite be said of the young Charles Albert, who teetered between the old law and the new.

4. The Light of the Spielberg

The Carbonarist movement in Lombardy differed from its Neapolitan counterpart, and was closer to the Piedmontese, in that it associated liberty, independence, and the kingdom of Northern Italy. The only apparent results of the Lombard-Venetian Carbonarist action were the Salvotti trials and the Spielberg. But the catastrophe was a triumph, prison an apotheosis. Martyrdom in the Spielberg, illuminated by the pure white light of *Le mie prigioni*, gave the cause of Italy a more solid and more powerful basis: that of offended and rebellious humanity. It aroused a new moral consciousness against positive law, proclaiming that legality is one thing and right is another, and that humanity is above governments and above "public order." Nothing was more legal than the Austrian political trials of those years; a man had only to deny everything to be absolved. If we consider the penal code, not even the punishments meted out were particularly severe. Everyone condemned to death had his sentence commuted to a term in prison, and was then set free after having served a few years. Nevertheless, the Italian and European moral conscience rebelled against the treatment of those patriots, those fighters for an ideal who were shut up in narrow, unhealthy, dark cells, with a bench as a bed, heavily chained, covered with such rough vestments as hair shirts, nourished, if one can use that word, on little and nauseating food, searched three times a day, deprived of books and of any activity other than chopping wood and darning socks.

The moral conscience rebelled, setting in motion a protest that Gladstone was to continue against the Bourbons after the middle of the century. An inhuman regime was by right a fallen regime; from this there was to be no appeal. Confalonieri turned out to be stronger than Metternich; Silvio Pellico judged Francis I. The divine right of governments and the old *ragion di stato* failed; clerical and papal support for the Austrian legal order was neutralized. The papal bull of September 13, 1821, had pronounced the excommunication of the Carbonari and those who failed to denounce them. That gave rise to some disgusting behavior on the part of a confessor at the Spielberg; and it signaled a clear moral separation between the Roman Curia and the human cause of the Italian patriots, a separation that was not to be bridged by Rome's refusal to condemn *Le mie prigioni*.

5. 1831 and 1833

The uprising of 1831 was in some ways similar to and in some ways different from 1821. It, too, was a regional upheaval; in fact, it consisted of many regional upheavals, and insisted on maintaining a regional character to the point of absurdity: witness the episode in which the Modenese, who were fleeing before the Austrians, were disarmed by the government of Bologna, who called them foreigners. Nevertheless, 1831 meant Central Italy was getting into the act, after Naples and Piedmont; the contagion of revolution was spreading over the whole peninsula. Although independence and liberty were not associated in 1831 as they had been in Piedmont in 1821, there was a step ahead in a different direction: instead of trying to impose a constitution on governments, the governments were simply deposed without further ado. Self-determination of the people was affirmed, though with some residue of the old law (appeal to the convention of 1447 between Bologna and Pope Nicholas V, violated by the popes). The idea of unity was even more glaringly absent in 1831 than it had been in '21; but there was a notable broadening of the insurrectionary social stratum: the bourgeoisie took the place of the army and the nobility, though the common people were not yet involved. Like '21, it had a European character, but of a different kind. Before the July Revolution, the French and the Italian liberals were linked through the Carbonarist conspiracy; but because the Italian revolution lagged a half year behind the French, the Italian rebels replaced the conspiratorial link with hope—in fact, faith in support from the new French government, founded on that government's proclamation of the policy of nonintervention. That gave rise to a miraculous sense of safety; and that sense was stronger than faith in themselves, in their own efforts. But the government resulting from the July Revolution now had its own conservative interests; and so we had the "betrayal" of Louis Philippe and the moderate leader Casimir Périer. France did not again take any revolutionary initiative in Italy until the time of the Second Empire; and that was good for Italian initiative, though for the time it represented a blow to European monarchical liberalism.

There was, to be sure, a modest French intervention in the Papal States, at Ancona, to counterbalance Austrian intervention in the Romagna. For a moment, it gave Italian liberals new hope for French support; but in reality the intervention was merely a small anticipation of 1849, a reinforcement of the Italian *ancien régime* rather than the beginning of something new. The only positive result of the French occupation of

Ancona was that it kept up the traditional French-Austrian rivalry in the peninsula. The earlier joint memorandum by the six powers (the five powers plus Sardinia) to the papal government, proposing reforms, was also devoid of essential results; but it accentuated, like 1821, the European character of the Italian problem.

The hopes of monarchical liberalism did not die even after the disappointment of '31, as is shown by the letter from Mazzini to Charles Albert. If the letter did not represent a personal conviction, a true faith in the king on the part of the new chief conspirator, it was nevertheless significant that Mazzini still felt it necessary to adapt himself in practice to that Carbonarist mentality which he was already beginning to combat in theory. As a matter of fact, the first period of Mazzinian action contains quite a few Carbonarist survivals, both ideologically and practically. It is particularly noteworthy that Mazzinian propaganda in Piedmont was directed mainly toward the army in the early years. The episodes of 1833 and 1834 can be connected to the earlier uprisings of 1821 and '31 for their military character, among other reasons.

The attitude of Charles Albert toward the revolutionaries was similar to that of Austria and the Bourbons; if anything, it was cruder. There have been recent attempts to justify him, symbolic of which is the attempt made on behalf of Galateri, who was nothing but a brutal and zealous chief of inquisitors and assassins. Attempts such as these, which attribute a historical-patriotic significance to Charles Albert's repression by saying that he saved the state that was to carry out the work of the Risorgimento, tend not only to revise but actually invert judgments pronounced during the Risorgimento. It remains to be seen whether Charles Albert's way was the only or the best way to save the state, and whether the manner and measure of the repression were necessary. For that purpose, the already mentioned comparison with Austria and the Bourbons is instructive. But the main point is that the whole apologetic argument rests on an abstract idealization of the state, and on a static, materialistic concept of the Savoyard monarchy. The monarchy of Victor Emmanuel II and Cavour, and even that of Charles Albert in 1848, are not the same as the monarchy of Charles Albert in 1833. And it is evident that if the new king had made even a gesture in the direction of the national-liberal program (as Mazzini had invited him to do), the attitude of the patriotic conspirators would have been different, just as it was later different toward the Charles Albert of 1848 and toward Victor Emmanuel II. Instead, the new king refused to grant amnesty to those condemned in 1821, despite the fact that he was undeniably linked to them, at least morally; he took no steps in a liberal-constitutional direction; and, worst of all, he concluded an alliance with Austria, and became the champion of pure legitimacy in France, Spain, and Portugal, outdoing Austria itself in retrogression. Except for Francis IV of Modena, no Italian sovereign took up the cause of reaction so completely. The Italian patriots of 1833 and 1834 and of the later years could not help but see in Charles Albert the incarnation of the anti-Risorgimento; they could not help but see deep truth (despite various factual errors, and despite the more balanced judgment that history can give today) in the famous quatrains of Giusti, showing Charles Albert genuflecting before Emperor Ferdinand of Austria, newly crowned king of Italy.

6. Political Immobility and Ideas in Motion

The fifteen-year period from the failure of the revolution of 1831 to the amnesty declared by Pius IX in 1846 is marked by an elaboration of the ideas that brought about the definitive work of the Risorgimento. That elaboration constitutes the main significance of the period, though the conspiracies and uprisings had their importance, too, in conformity with the Mazzinian principle of "thought and action." However little or much there was of action, it served as a touchstone for the thought. Three currents are clearly distinguishable: Mazzinianism, moderate liberalism, and radical liberalism (or republican federalism). They have in common their reflection on the immediate past and on present Italian and European realities, for the purpose of correcting the insufficiencies of the earlier uprisings, and pointing out the paths for the future. And they had some results in common, too: emphasis of the ideological-ethical character of the Risorgimento as opposed to a purely political movement; examination of the problem in all its aspects, with each contributing in a different way to the formation of a national consciousness and a national program; and placing the Italian problem before the conscience of Europe.

The Italian governments, and indeed all governments, remained outside this process of elaboration; their actions never went beyond administrative improvements or paternalistic provisions. This negative assessment is opposed by a thesis that goes back to the semiofficial historiography of the Risorgimento written after the unification, and very loudly proclaimed in recent times. The thesis states that the work of Charles Albert in the first fifteen years of his reign prepared the way for subsequent patriotic action. Once again, such a thesis seems irremediably tainted with materialism. It supposes that because the work of royal reform fortified the Savoyard state—which is to say, furnished it with the material means for the national enterprise—it ought to be judged as genuine, direct, and primary preparation for the Risorgimento. We would then see perfect continuity between Charles Albert the ally of Austria and the Charles Albert of Goito. (Nor does this interpretation pay much attention to the constitution.) But means must be consonant with ends, for they are ends themselves; the banal doctrine that the end justifies the means does not understand that. One must look for the spirit inside matter.

Of Charles Albert's activity in that fifteen-year period, we can say in particular what we have said in general about the works of the Restoration princes: it was a resumption of eighteenth-century enlightened absolutism, and therefore tainted with anachronism. Worse than anachronistic was the political-moral education of the ruling classes, both civilian and military. They were removed, segregated from all ideas of liberty and self-government, ideas inseparable from and essential to the national cause; they clung to throne and altar, in close solidarity with the Europe of the Congress of Vienna, and were oriented toward Austria, the main support of that Europe and of throne and altar. It has been very opportunely recalled that for years officers at the artillery and engineers academy in Turin heard one of their professors exalting the Holy Alliance and the treaties of Vienna, and vilifying not only the French Revolution but the Piedmontese upheavals of 1821 as well. This complete political reaction went together with the caste exclusiveness of the aristocratic ruling class, which was distinctly separate from the bourgeoisie; and the whole thing was crowned by the mortification and subjection of culture by the Jesuits and Sanfedisti. Cavour (despite his hostility toward revolutionaries and Mazzinianism) called the Turin of that time an "intellectual hell," and Massimo d'Azeglio, who was even more moderate than Cavour, confessed that in order to breathe he occasionally went to Milan, which was under Austria. When texts such as these are obliterated, we can talk of changing the judgment on the history of those fifteen years in the reign of Charles Albert.

7. Mazzinianism

The three currents developed almost contemporaneously. The first to rise and grow was Mazzinianism, and the first manifestations of radical liberalism precede those of moderate liberalism by a few years. But because moderate liberalism was in large part a conscious reaction to Mazzinianism, we shall examine it second; and last we will look at radical liberalism, which opposed both the moderates and the Mazzinians.

Mazzini's thought was already fully formed and widely propagated before 1840, through his writings in Young Italy, through his pamphlets, and through his very numerous letters, which were so rich in life and thought, and so effective and intense as instruments of propaganda; the systematic expression of moderate and radical liberalism, on the other hand, came after 1840. Let it be understood that we are examining these currents not as pure political thought, but rather as they contributed to the course of the Risorgimento. (Of course, a completely clear-cut separation of the two aspects is not really possible.)

Mazzini started with criticism of the Carbonarist movement. He reproached Carbonarist liberalism for looking only at humanity and individuals, for ignoring the nation and society, for taking no account of the people, and for being utilitarian rather than moral by affirming only rights and not duties. He extended his criticism to the entire liberal movement that had emerged from the French Revolution. The French origin of that liberalism played a role (at least as a psychological factor in his criticism), for Mazzini's national passion had always made him jealous of French initiative; it was precisely the French Revolution that gave birth to the modern concept of the nation in all its power and dominance, subordinating the individual even to the point of sacrificing him completely. Nevertheless, Mazzini was correct in energetically emphasizing the national-social element, which Carbonarist liberalism had ignored. But he was not equally correct, even vis-à-vis Carbonarism, in the negative part of his criticism; i.e., in the assignment of a partial and instrumental value to liberty. Mazzini was rather hastily inclined to consider liberty as something preliminary, a presupposition which it was no longer necessary to think about because it was already attained, at least ideally. Nor did he ever succeed, perhaps, in comprehending the concept of liberty in all its positive, final, synthetic value, all of which is revealed if one takes (as one should take) liberty to mean the full development of the human personality. Mazzini was so intent on his ideas of association, solidarity, and duty that he failed to see the full scope and nature of this concept of personality. The collective idea of nation and society, which was not completely devoid of mythology, obscured his mind somewhat. In that respect, the radicals and even the moderates were superior to him. Nevertheless, if we look well, we will see that the fundamental Mazzinian concept of the limitless progress of humanity was nothing but a different formulation of the need for personal development. Individual man serves humanity; but "humanity is simply the ladder by which man moves closer to God." The two terms fuse at the boundary; the ultimate future of the individual is identical with that of humanity.

Whatever one may think of the nature of Mazzini's concept of liberty and its imperfections, the fact remains that for him the term fatherland, or nation, is inseparable from the term liberty. He once wrote, with his characteristic uncertainty of expression: "I love liberty, I love it perhaps more than I love my fatherland; but I love my fatherland before I love liberty." The "before" balances the "more," and vice versa. The need for liberty and for institutions based on liberty are at the base of his national structure. To be sure, more than any other Italian writer of the time, he rejects the eighteenth-century tendency to conceive of society as a simple aggregate or sum of individuals; and he places the nation as an organic whole at the center of his conception of the Risorgimento. But for him the nation is the people, the whole people willing to take its destinies into its own hands, rather than entrust them to a privileged class or individual. The concept of popular initiative, of national action and self-government, is fundamental for Mazzini: it may be called the alpha and omega of his political system.

In this organic and dynamic conception of the Italian nation as the self-creation of the people resides one of Mazzini's major contributions to the course of the Risorgimento, both in theory and in practice. That conception gave birth to the Mazzinian binomial "thought and action," both terms of which he considered necessary for a true national consciousness. For Mazzini, the Italian nation has a past, a present, and above all a future. He does not consider the Italian past something to be brought back, to be restored "in its former state," a model to be copied; rather, he sees it as a stimulus, an auspice, to be used to get out of the present depths and to get on with the reconstruction of Italy. Reconstruction or, rather, construction: for if Mazzini appeals to ancient republican-imperial Rome and to papal-medieval Rome, dominators and mistresses of the world, and in their name invokes and prophesies a Third Rome, he does not speak with the same precision of a first and second Italy, to be succeeded by a third. Rather, he sees in the new Italian nation the necessary condition for a Third Rome; and at the same time, in a sort of circular process, he sees in the fact of an Italian Rome a particularly powerful foundation for the future mission of Italy.

The concept of national mission is one of Mazzini's fundamental ideas—one might even be tempted to call it an *idée fixe*; but it is also one of his vaguest ideas. Each nation has a special task to perform; but what it is, for Italy or the other nations, Mazzini does not say (until very late, and then only a little). Briefly, what duty is for the individual, mission is for the nation; but Mazzini seems not to have quite noticed that duty-mission cannot be something stable, something determined a priori, something specific and reserved to an individual or a collectivity; duties and missions always spring forth anew and different from the variety of situations. Nor can a mission consist of a "principle" of which a single nation is the privileged interpreter; for if it is really a matter of principles—that is to say, of essential elements—they will all be necessary to each nation. As a matter of fact, the only mission Mazzini defines for Italy is that of initiating the resurrection and confederation of the peoples, a mission that corresponded to the the historical situation of the time, and one that any nation could have taken on, given the proper circumstances. Still, his faith in that exalted Italian mission was very useful for awakening and developing national energies, and for identifying the Italian cause with that of all the other nations. That identification was underlined by Mazzini himself, the creator of Young Europe, the man in constant contact with other European national movements.

As we have already pointed out, the Mazzinian concept of nation contains a remnant of sociological mythology. But that must not hide the vital nucleus, which resides in a moral, ideal concept of the nation rather than in a purely territorial-political concept. Mazzini's concept represents the conscious hope of re-establishing the moral unity in Italian life that had begun to disappear with the Renaissance (cf. above, p. 18). Any form of statist materialism is incompatible with the Mazzinian spirit. For him, Italy is a historical tradition; even more, it is a moral life, a spirit, a vocation to the service of humanity; and the Italian unity invoked by Mazzini is a moral need, a spiritual reality. Territorial unity is an instrument for the gathering of moral forces, and for the explication of national solidarity; it is a sensible manifestation of the unity of consciences, the just realization of the will of the people. The idea of creating Italy by having one state politically and militarily absorb the other existing states was repugnant to Mazzini, no less than it was to the republican federalists (though for other reasons). And what is true for unity is also true for the republic: Mazzini does not consider it to be simply one form of government as opposed to others—on the same plane, for example, with a constitutional monarchy; nor does he consider it merely an explication of the principle of liberty (as it was for the republican federalists). Rather, it is the unity of conscience and action, the necessary coronation of the national structure, the indispensable instrument for the national mission. All this is reinforced by the historical traditions of the grandiose Italian past, which for Mazzini are republican, not monarchical.

The ideal, moral value of the unified Italian republic was to realize itself above all in its social content. Mazzini felt the social problem very acutely for Italy as for the rest of Europe. If he fought against the communist solution (which in his eyes was marred by utopianism, antiliberalism, and above all materialism), his social requirements were no less radical than those of socialism. For him, the principle of equality required that each man, by virtue of his work, participate in the enjoyment of the products of social activity. One day, Mazzini says, we shall all be workers, we will live by our own work. In the social problem, too, Mazzini considers that initiative and action belong to the people themselves and to the popular state. Any kind of paternalism, corporate or otherwise, is foreign to his thought. The formulation and the attempted solution of the social problem represent the superiority of Mazzini to moderate liberalism, which practically ignored the problem. (It is energetically posed by Gioberti in the *Rinnovamento*; but by then Gioberti is well beyond moderatism.)

The concept of humanity coordinates—or, better still, rises above—the concept of nation, and crowns its ideal character. It places an insurmountable barrier, a veritable abyss, between Mazzinianism and any kind of national ethnicism. He is not concerned with making one nation—Italy—dominant, but with building a world of nations. If he repeatedly attributes to Italy the mission of being the initiator (the people-Christ), the mission is political-spiritual, not political-territorial; and it is to be carried out by means that conform to the moral law, in brotherhood with all peoples, and through joint action of all "the good." The individual national causes are indissolubly conjoined among themselves, and together they will triumph against the governments through the associated efforts of the peoples. This is European Mazzinianism, foreign and opposed to all diplomacy and to any combination of particularistic interests of governments or dynasties.

Every nationalistic conception presupposes the primacy of politics over any other activity of the spirit. The Mazzinian conception of the Risorgimento, on the other hand, completely overcomes the political through the spiritual. Not only is all *ragion di stato* radically rejected, but politics is integrally subordinated to ethics; and ethics is nothing but the application of religious faith. Mazzini took up the Italian religious problem, with a view toward a radical solution. Here we touch the true depths of the Mazzinian revolution. It does not reside in a political rearrangement (which might allow for gradualness and expediency); nor does it reside in insurrection, which is a simple temporary instrument; rather, his revolution resides in this inner religious transformation. He speaks explicitly of a new faith, which goes not only beyond the old Christian confessions he now considers impotent, but also beyond the skeptical and materialist nonbelief of the eighteenth century. He clearly rejects the efforts of the Italian neo-Catholics or neo-Guelphs: their school, according to him, is of no use to Italian progress, for it misunderstands the idea of Italian progress by preaching a faith it does not really feel. There is no place in the Mazzinian Risorgimento for the papacy and for Catholicism. That does not mean, naturally, that he was thinking of having them forcibly abolished or persecuted, for nothing could be farther from his thought. It simply means he did not attribute any positive function to them. Mazzini even considered Christianity itself exhausted, not because it was false, but because the truth in it (individual redemption) had already triumphed. What remains necessary is otherworldly faith, which for him is faith in God, who manifests himself to humanity through successive revelations; one day, all humanity will be called up to God, just as individuals ascend to him in their successive lives. Until such time as social unity is estab-

lished, ecclesiastical and political authority must remain as independent of each other as possible. But once the new society
has really been constituted, there will be no more reason for
the separation of Church and state, or of political and religious institutions. Ethics will conform to faith, and will be
realized in politics; so, too, the state shall be the Church, and
the Church shall be the state. No divorce between heaven and
earth; our work on this earth is a sacred task, the realization
of the reign of God.

According to Mazzini, the path toward this ideal must go
through national education, which has the task of making all
the men of one nation feel like brothers, of taking them from
the isolation in which they find themselves, of imbuing them
with the same beliefs and the same spirit, and of making possible a full development of their faculties, overcoming the conditions of social inferiority in which so many of them live.
This education is the task of the social authority; it is to be
public, political-moral instruction, of a uniform character.
Such a conception could have heavy consequences; but it is
substantially corrected, or integrated, by what Mazzini says
about the coexistence of national education and free instruction. To the first belongs the teaching of social duty and the
national program; to the second the free diffusion of new programs and of new ideals which assure freedom of progress,
protected and promoted by the state.

For Mazzini, then, the formation of moral unity is something gradual, not something sudden; free, not imposed; and,
given continuous progress, it is never finished. It is up to the
people to interpret and apply this moral unity. When compared with authoritarians and moderates, the fundamental
point in Mazzini is that the new government must be not only
for the people, but by the people. He ascribes a general political capacity to the people, which is that of spontaneously
choosing the most capable. He does not allow that national
and popular politics can be embodied in dominating individ-

uals: one may not attribute to individuals an authority that
belongs only to principles. A nation must not make momen-
tary use of its freedom of choice only to abandon it again;
rather, it must so organize its institutions as to allow the continued exercise of its liberty and sovereignty, securing them so
fast that they will not be lost by the mistake of an individual
or a dynasty.

All this is a counterbalance—and up to a certain point an
overcoming—of the danger implicit in Mazzini's mystical reduction of politics to religion: the danger, namely, that with
one of those upsets that can take place so easily in intellec-
tually or morally weak spirits, politics—and therefore the contingent utility of a given situation, or of a particular program,
institution, or party—would be raised to morality, imposed
from above, and consecrated in immobility. To be sure, the
danger is not completely overcome, because his mysticism ignores necessary distinctions. Nor can it be denied that his conception of the Risorgimento contains a residue of dogmatism
and transcendence, which his contemporaries and even his followers felt very keenly. Open opposition or inner repugnance
to it were among the most grave obstacles to the effectiveness
of Mazzini's action. Radical liberalism, with its absolute
humanism devoid of all transcendence, found it particularly
offensive; and moderate liberalism, with its realistic and empirical sense, opposed it, too. And in their opposition they
both combined the traditions of eighteenth-century thought
(which Mazzini had not fully understood) with the new his-
torical-scientific thought.

Still, Mazzini may boast the most integral conception of the
Risorgimento, the one that most closely associated thought
and action without any sterile ideological dilettantism. He also
associated political resurrection with moral elevation, uproot-
ing all Machiavellism; and he associated the fate of Italy with
the fate of all Europe, thereby cutting off any attempts at
isolation, any claim to dominion. If the Risorgimento of the

Italian people required the ability to rise out of the spiritual abysses to which they had been led by the centuries of decadence following the Renaissance, the moral push for that rise came mainly from the mystical afflatus of Mazzini. There was no one else among the patriotic propagandists of the Risorgimento who threw forth as many threads as did Mazzini, wove as many plots, illuminated and excited as many spirits, formed and held together as many nuclei of action, appealed to so many different groups, put his hand to so many different instruments. In brief, there was no one else who spent all his intelligence, all his energies, his every breath for the cause of Italy and humanity.

8. *Moderate Liberalism*

The moderatism of Balbo, Azeglio, the early Gioberti, and others was not only politically inspired, but rooted in culture as well. It was closely linked to the reflowering of historical studies, particularly to the study of Italian history. In Italy, eighteenth-century erudition was fructified in the first half of the next century by the new historical-national consciousness, which in turn was nourished by the spirit of humanity and sociality inherited from the eighteenth century. One can say that the study of Italian history gave birth to the moderate school; Manzoni, Troya, Capponi, and Balbo show that clearly. The one great exception is the philosopher-orator Gioberti, and even he is only a partial exception because he, too, was nourished on historical studies (though his mentality cannot really be called historical). In fact, he claimed to have based his *Primato* on historical foundations. It would not be easy to find a period in the history of another nation in which the political and cultural movements are as closely associated as they are in the Risorgimento—unassailable evidence fatal to all those purely territorial-political interpretations of the Risorgimento.

The study of national history was cultivated not only by eminent individuals, but by organizations as well, such as the *Deputazione di Storia Patria* founded by Charles Albert at Turin, and even more by the *Archivio Storico Italiano*, founded privately by Vieusseux, who was of Swiss origin, and who had also started the *Antologia* earlier. The institution of a chair of Italian history by Charles Albert at the University of Turin in 1846 may be pointed out as one of the signs of the direction of his development.

The study of national history produced two results for the Risorgimento: a better knowledge of the Italian past, with lessons and auspices for the future; and a clearer consciousness of the relations between Italy and Europe, with a better view of the European aspect of the Italian problem. The national and the European elements were still tied together. The Risorgimento could not fail to be strongly nourished by the reminder and the recounting of the past greatness of Italy, while the analysis of its decadence pointed out the difficulties and the means to overcome them. A strong political element came into the choice and the evaluation of the various historical periods. It has already been clearly pointed out by a renowned teacher that a whole school of Italian historians, who were also patriots and moderates or neo-Guelph or Catholic-liberal or what-have-you politicians, concentrated not on ancient Rome (in this, too, there was a difference between Mazzini and the moderates), and not even on the Renaissance, but on the Middle Ages, on the age of the communes. The values they extracted from Italian history were independence and liberty rather than unity of the state. Balbo, as is well known, gave absolute precedence to independence over liberty. One might even say he made it exclusive, to the point of requiring that the passion for independence extinguish all other national passions (*"porro unum est necessarium,"* according to the epigraph in his *Speranze d'Italia,* which his religious scruples later caused him to remove). But in that he was alone even within the moderate school. Durando polemicized openly against him, though without mentioning his name, saying that it was a grave error to maintain that one should think only of independence and not worry about liberty: an Italian political reordering in a constitutional direction was the only way to obtain a moral focalization of the nation. Balbo himself, for that matter, was talking about opportunities, not about principles; so far as past history is concerned, he is second to none in giving prominence to liberty as the root of our most splendid civilizations.

The knowledge of Italian and European history, coupled with an examination of present reality, clearly revealed to these political researchers the process of decadence Italy had gone through after the beginning of the modern age, at a time when other European nations were moving upward. The general goal, therefore, was to raise Italy to the level of European civilization. For they did believe in a common European or Christian civilization, which constituted the link between and the value of modern nations. To participate in this civilization was the fundamental, foremost condition of life for each nation. The very Italian Balbo insisted more doggedly—one might even say more crudely—than anyone else that present-day Italy was inferior when compared to the other nations; he censured the boasting of past Italian glories, which induced dreams of an irretrievable Italian past and distracted men's minds from present reality. Italy could not isolate itself from European life; it could only occupy one of the last places in it, at least for a while. The primary reasons for its inferiority were its present inexperience, and its meager contribution to representative government, in which Balbo saw the greatest political progress of Europe.

The same Europeanism was reached through another branch of studies, which comes immediately after history in order of importance for the Risorgimento. These were economic-technical studies, whose principal organs included such Lombard periodicals as Romagnosi's *Annali Universali di Statistica* and Cattaneo's *Politecnico*. We shall speak of Cattaneo's politics soon; but here we must mention that these studies nourished modern thought and the formation of a reform program by favoring the development of industries, construction of railroads, the lowering of duties, and customs unions. The same can be said of the congresses of Italian scientists. Generally, they were trying to bring national energies into play and to develop them in all fields by associating them with one another in their various forms, and in the various regions, in the clear knowledge that all this meant building the new Italy. The most important assertions in the field of economics (assertions which also had a political and national value) were made by the statesman who was to take moderatism to its supreme heights, then rise above it by allying himself with the revolution: Camillo di Cavour. Europeanism was a fundamental characteristic of Cavour's thought even before 1848. The common European civilization of which we spoke earlier led Cavour to call the various peoples of Europe "branches of the great Christian family"; and the problem of rejoining Italy to European civilization was another spur to his Europeanism. Like the other moderates, or even more so, Cavour kept his eyes fixed especially on England and France. Balbo was also expressing one of Cavour's fundamental thoughts when he spoke of "Anglo-French civilization, the civilization of Western Europe," as being identical with "progressing civilization."

A unique exception to the Europeanism of the moderates is Gioberti, at the time of the *Primato*. Unique, and at first sight impressive, because the common notion is that his book founded the moderate school and was its gospel. It is a common notion, but it is wrong, for it confuses the moderate ideological process with the fortunes of moderatism in Italian public opinion. The *Primato* broke Italian silence. It reconciled to the national movement a number of elements that had hitherto been aloof or hostile; but it was far from being representative of the thought common to the moderate school. Reactionary and utopian elements are closely associated in the *Primato*. In the tone, if not in the recondite intentions of the author, there is a basically negative criticism of modern civilization. The destinies of Italy—and, in fact, of European civilization—are placed in the hands of the pope and clergy; Italian primacy is rhetorically exalted not only as past reality or possible future but as virtual present. The other men of his school disagreed with Gioberti on all these points, sometimes even with jokes and irony. And he himself hastened to reinterpret his thought—that is to say, to abandon it, accepting the European positions of the others.

The moderate political program for a new Italy also consisted of an association of national and European characteristics. From an examination of the nation's past and present, they deduced their monarchical federalism. They established the reality of the different Italian states formed gradually through the centuries, and they proposed to preserve them by reforming them on the model of the most advanced European states. Their task was to build on what they had: "The only good change is to progress from present to future things" (Balbo). Their historical criterion was counterbalanced by their moderate political criterion: their desire to produce the minimum amount of confusion possible for Italy and for European civilization; their fear of popular initiative; and the theoretical negation of and practical aversion to democracy. (This negation, however, was not the only or the last word of the school, for Balbo as well as Cavour spoke of a final democratic victory.) England and France furnished the model for the constitutional-monarchical arrangement envisioned for each of the Italian states.

The significance of the moderate national program for the Risorgimento consisted in the propagation of the national idea among large sections which would otherwise have remained foreign to it; in bringing together political, economic, cultural, and religious forces to work for the Risorgimento; in showing that it was possible to have an immediate minimum program without revolution; and in bringing the conservative forces and the governments of Europe closer to the Italian cause.

9. Radical Liberalism

Cattaneo and Ferrari had not developed their political program openly or completely before 1848; but when it came, it was completely imbued with the spirit they had manifested in their earlier writings. Cattaneo's *Interdizioni israelitiche*, written in 1835, already reveals his whole mentality, a mentality that found ample occasion to express itself in his collaboration with the *Annali di Statistica* (which began in 1832), and above all in the editing of the *Politecnico* from 1839 to 1844. Ferrari's *La mente di Giandomenico Romagnosi*, written in 1835, already contains elements very characteristic of his thought; he then further unfolds his ideas in his writings published in France, in French, between 1843 and 1848. The first contradictions of Mazzini came from them, not from the moderates.

Through Cattaneo, who was far more levelheaded than the chaotic and paradoxical Ferrari, radical liberalism is closely linked to the scientific-technical thought of the time, to which we have repeatedly referred. One can say that the scientific-positive framework of radical liberalism corresponds to the historical-literary framework of moderate liberalism, though the latter element was not lacking among the radicals, just as we have seen the former element in the moderates. Particularly noteworthy is the re-evaluation of the Middle Ages common to both groups, though the spirit behind the re-evaluation is somewhat different. Both groups were formed of thinkers rather than men of action, very different from Mazzini's thought-and-action bloc. They were not inclined to mix with the multitude, even though the multitude formed an integral part of the theoretical program (at least in the case of the radicals). Both groups—here again in contrast to Mazzini—wanted to build on the present, on that which already existed, and proceed in an evolutionary, not revolutionary, manner. Ferrari and Cattaneo, no less than the moderates, were ready to accept and even to promote reforms by the governments in the individual states. In fact, Cattaneo, on the eve of the Five Days, was still ready to go along with Austria, counting on an evolution toward federalism in the Hapsburg Empire. The federalism of the moderates and radicals has a common point of departure in this acceptance of present reality, in this adoption of the method of reform. Also, both were against secret societies and conspiracies. Both had a positive, rational mentality that loved distinctions, in contrast to the ardent unific mysticism of Mazzini.

But here the similarities end and the differences begin. For the moderates, reform is an end in itself, a point of arrival; it means the modified preservation of the present. For the radicals, reform is simply the instrument of a progressively unfolding revolution. The federalism of the moderates signifies respect for existing sovereignties; that of the radicals is a full, true guarantee for the realization of liberty and popular sovereignty, to be erected on the ruins of existing sovereignties. The one group consists of Catholic Christians, the other of positivist scientists and freethinkers. For the moderates, the Risorgimento is essentially a monarchical-constitutional reordering brought about by the governments, and the elimination of foreign domination; for the radicals, it is total liberation, political, social, and above all intellectual. Their radicalism is more ideological than political; it inspires the reforms to be made within existing institutions, so that even when they agree with the moderates on the material content of those reforms, they are imbued with a very different spirit. When the radicals confront traditional institutions and traditional beliefs, they empty out the former and reject the latter. The light of science and reason—that is their guide. For them, science and culture are the supreme values; they know of no metaphysical or religious transcendence. For them, the state is a creation of the intelligence. Cattaneo is not really thinking of the political association of the peoples envisioned by Mazzini, but of the international association of intellects.

This universal affinity founded on reason negates nationalism in its root, and goes far beyond the Europeanism of the moderates. It is not a question of putting Italy at the head of the peoples for a European mission, but of having the light of science and reason, which already covers the rest of Europe, shine fully on our country. Cattaneo knows nothing of particular missions of peoples, while Ferrari credits democratic France with having initiated progress and the European revolution. But what is important for both men is the free development of all associated individuals, which is similar everywhere. For the moderates, liberty reduced itself to a collection of juridical institutions that guaranteed particular freedoms; for Mazzini, it was a presupposition and an instrument for social solidarity, the new national edifice, and the association of the peoples; for Ferrari and Cattaneo, it was the foremost value, containing all others. The point Balbo made in favor of independence is turned around by them in favor of liberty. Ferrari even speaks of an opposition between liberty and independence, citing Piedmontese absolutism to prove his point. Even after '48, he maintains that we must make war against our native servitude before fighting the foreigner. For these men, liberty has religious value; it is their new religion, explicitly proclaimed as such. Ferrari rejects the ancient religion (with particular harshness after 1848), considering it the principal foundation of the old order that must disappear, whereas Cattaneo prefers to ignore it. Basing himself on Kant, Ferrari proclaims the need for a universal Church over and above the state; and it turns out to be the association of rational minds of which Cattaneo spoke.

The nation is by no means ignored in this rational cosmopolitanism; rather, it is looked upon as a new creation of European and world civilization, and not as a reality handed down from the past. Nevertheless, Ferrari, who is more historically-minded than Cattaneo, connects this conception with the conception of the Risorgimento as Italy's resumption of the progressive work it had begun long ago, and which was then continued by other countries. One of his fundamental ideas is that the rebirth of Europe began in Italy with the communes, and was continued with the Renaissance; then it passed to Germany with the Reformation, and to France with the Revolution; now Italy had to regain what it had allowed to escape. This conception is historically founded and ideally integral, like the one that connects cultural, religious, and political development without confusing them. At the same time it, too, restores Italian moral unity, in a form different from that of Mazzini.

In this conception, Italian history and European history, Italian rebirth and European development, formed an organic circle. Ferrari was obsessed by the idea (an obsession that did nothing to enhance his fame) of the indissoluble connection between the Italian Risorgimento and French politics, derived from the fact that he considered France the incarnation of revolution—a viewpoint rendered plausible by 1789, 1830, and 1848. Ferrari was not just looking at France; he was looking at progressive and revolutionary France. He thought Italy could most properly take up its inheritance by allying itself with France and receiving her support. Ferrari-Cattaneo and the *Primato* of Gioberti represent a maximum antithesis: the former wanted the complete assimilation of old Italy into new Europe; the latter envisioned, or said he envisioned, the reduction of new Europe to old Italy. In the *Rinnovamento*, Gioberti accepted in substance the conception of Ferrari by making national Italian fulfillment depend on the expansion of the democratic movement.

At this point, the federalism of the two thinkers appears in its true light, even as compared with Mazzini; and it appears not as moderatism but as radicalism. They do not want a unitary state embracing all of Italy, because they consider it an imposition from outside and above, to the detriment of the various Italian peoples, whose free development it would impede. Republican federalism assures popular initiative, and local and individual liberties. The monarchical federalism of the moderates and the republican federalism of Ferrari and Cattaneo are completely antithetical: they represent a minimum and a maximum of liberty, of upheaval, and of modernity. Liberty and unity, Cattaneo said, can only be coupled as they are in Switzerland and the United States; to preserve liberty, the people must keep their hands on it. In Ferrari, there is also a distinct social note, which after '48 becomes antireligious. Pisacane later gave that note its maximum development, when he postulated socialism as the objective of the Italian revolution. Italian federalism fit itself into the European—and, in fact, the world—framework, for Cattaneo had his eye on the British Empire and on America. He described the universal upheaval of the peoples reborn, each of them reconquering its own consciousness, and understanding that the liberty of each nation was the necessary condition for the liberty of all the others.

10. National Convergence

So far as theory is concerned, the differences among the three schools are perhaps greater than the agreements. But here we must evaluate them historically, in the actual concreteness of the Risorgimento. If we do that, they will appear to us to be complementary. In the moderates, we find the sense and the knowledge of the real, and the political technique for using that knowledge; in the radicals, we have a clear statement of liberal, innovating, and liberating ideas; in Mazzini, we have the moral and religious spirit, the apostolicity of propaganda, the mystical unity of thought and action. If we wanted to characterize each of the three schools with one word, we might say: politics, thought, and faith; or, independence, liberty, and solidarity. The simultaneous flow of these three currents produced grandiose results: each of these very different points of view aroused the intelligence and the sentiments of Italians, and reached very diverse strata of national society. The Italian problem was posed in all its aspects, in Italy and abroad; all the national forces were awakened, excited, mobilized. There was action that risked life and liberty, as in the case of the heroic sacrifice of the Bandiera brothers, or in the uprising at Rimini, which was a very significant effort made by moderate reform to realize its goals through insurrection. And another result was that Italian national forces were joined with those of other nations.

It is often said that the Risorgimento was the work of a minority. We must be clear about what that means. The active political role is always played by the minority, because the majority has other things to do. It has the task of daily work, of assuring the continuity of life, without which the superior work of the minority could not exist. To have a Magdalen to light the lamp of the spirit, there must be a Martha to take care of the household chores. What we must look at is the relationship between the minority that leads and the majority that follows: is it one of persuasion or compulsion, of inner participation or passive adherence, in the light of consciousness or in the shadows of ignorance? The minority that made the Risorgimento belonged to the first type, which is the only one that can build lasting edifices. And that was due precisely to the three schools, which furnished a sound and profound ideal basis for the political movement of the Risorgimento such as few other political movements can boast. Those currents of thought were not a preparation, an occasion, or an aid for the Risorgimento; they were its very soul, which found its body in the conspiracies, insurrections, wars, popular demonstrations, plebiscites, and parliamentary votes. Only the impressiveness of that movement of thought can explain the proportions suddenly assumed by the popular Italian resurgence from 1846 to 1848, which seemed to be the sudden flaring of an enormous fire; and after the failure, only it can explain the resumption, and the rapid and sweeping ultimate success.

CHAPTER V

The National Revolution

1. The Physiognomy of 1848

The European revolution of 1848 has a prologue in the Italian reform movement of 1846–47; the Sicilian revolution of January, 1848, comes between them. It is an insufficiently recognized fact that the reform movement had a plainly pre-revolutionary character. The reforms, to be sure, were carried out by the sovereigns, but under the immediate and continual pressure of the people. To that extent, it was very different from the reform movement of the eighteenth century. Now, throughout the entire peninsula, the "town square" was broadly and systematically mobilized—something which King Charles Albert found very repugnant. So did Count Balbo, who condemned the people's use and abuse of demonstrations in one of his doctrinaire-polemical writings, so lively and il-luminating even when they are wrong. His aristocratic-con-servative temperament did not permit Balbo to understand that the gatherings in the squares were neither good nor evil in themselves. Everything depended on what was in and behind them: whether they were an effective movement of minds and wills, occasional disorderly ephemeral tumults, or, for that matter, simply parades on command, to promote plebiscitary, Jacobin, or Napoleonic (and today we might add

Fascistic or totalitarian) illusions. Whatever else one may say about those disturbances in the squares between 1846 and 1848 (and to a certain extent they are inseparable from any popular movement), they were, on the whole, physiological manifestations of a new, or renewed, organism, coming forth to fresh life. And if '48 failed, the failure was not due to those disturbances, but to the absence or scarcity of other factors. (One might even say that the failure of '48 was in part due to the lack or weakness of the sort of popular agitation that had manifested itself in those very disturbances.) Such disturbances were a natural result of all the preceding elaboration of thought and of the diverse propaganda (including even that of the moderates), all of which would have been useless if it had not reached the people and had not promoted their active participation. Now one could hardly expect popular participation to be as orderly and discreet as a convention of scientists or an academic assembly.

The popular uprisings of 1846–48 represent not only the effect but the convergence of the three currents of thought we have delineated. The initial program was that of the moderates, carried out (in conformity with moderate principles) by the governments; but it was carried out under popular pressure, in keeping with the need for national initiative propounded by Mazzini, though not in ways he liked. The upheavals took place autonomously in the various states, and led to the transformation of each state, just as the republican federalists wanted. Later developments led from the moderate program to the Mazzinian and radical program. In 1848, we have *l'Italia farà da sè*, the connection with the insurrection of other peoples, and the intervention of European diplomacy; we have action on the part of governments, the enlightened bourgeoisie, and the people; we have Guelphs and Ghibellines, federalists and unitarians, liberals, democrats, and socialists. The Italian revolution of 1848 repeated 1796–99, 1821, and

1831, and prepared the way for 1859–70. Yet it had a physiognomy all its own, and it was the most comprehensive upheaval of all.

2. *The Triumph of Neo-Guelphism*

This entire grandiose movement began with a modest, almost banal event: the political amnesty granted by Pope Pius IX to solemnize his advent to the throne. If not really banal, the event can at least be called normal. Eight years earlier, Emperor Ferdinand I of Austria had granted a general amnesty at the time of his royal coronation at Milan. The predecessors of Pius IX had also granted amnesties on similar occasions, though their scope was smaller. Moreover, the amnesty of Pius IX was subject to a humiliating condition: the manifesto spoke of "forgiveness" and ended with a threat to be carried out in case the pope's hopes in the effects of this forgiveness should prove vain. The grandiose results of the act derived from two circumstances: it came in a situation loaded with novel elements, and it came from the pope. The amnesty was taken as a sign of change in papal politics. The whole political-religious problem of the Risorgimento seemed to be posed in new terms. What had hitherto been an obstacle seemed to become the most powerful moving force.

Until then, there had been a threefold opposition between the papacy and the Risorgimento. First: the papacy had anointed the legitimacy of governments with the sacred oil of religion. The altar had placed itself in front of the throne, so that it seemed necessary to topple the one to get at the other; and that was frightful and inconceivable to Italian public opinion, composed as it was almost entirely of believers— or, if not believers, at least people respectful of the religious national tradition. Second point: while the papacy was consecrating the legitimacy of absolute governments, it condemned liberal principles; that is to say, it prohibited its subjects from asking for changes in a liberal direction, even through regular channels, and it prohibited governments from granting them. Already in 1832, the encyclical of Gregory XVI, *Mirari vos*, directed against Lamennais, had formally pronounced the condemnation that was later to be codified in the *Syllabus* of Pius IX. Although Lamennais (who had followers in Italy, too) was condemned and left the Church, liberal Catholicism was nevertheless reborn in France after 1840. However, it wavered between opportunism and affirmation of principle; it was confessionalistic in practical attitudes (defense of the Jesuits), and yet suspect in its doctrinal orthodoxy.

In any case, that was a French affair, rooted in the ecclesiastical politics of France. Our liberal Catholicism was neo-Guelphism. By studying the history of Italy, it had tried to show that in the Middle Ages the papacy was intimately connected with the history of the nation, and had favored Italian independence and liberty. It remained to be seen whether the same thing could happen now; and in this connection the two obstacles we mentioned above presented themselves. There was a third obstacle, which seemed to be the greatest of all: the temporal power of the pope. It, too, was a "legitimate" government, but in addition it was "sacred," a feature which the pope and the clergy in the Middle Ages had conferred upon everything that pertained to themselves. If a feudal right or a territorial possession belonged to ecclesiastics, it became a *noli me tangere*, little less than the articles of the Credo. Connected with this sacred character was the concept of the Church as a "perfect society," to which material possessions and coercive powers belonged as an integral part of its make-up. Naturally, the papal government could not allow in its own house those liberal principles (religious tolerance, freedom of the press) which it condemned abroad. Because of their anti- or non-Catholicism, the Mazzinians and the radicals got rid of this obstacle by simply not allowing any place for the papacy in the Italian future. Not so the moderates, who, in accord with general national opinion, made a fundamental point of the preservation of the papacy in the framework of the nation. They also supported, therefore, the preservation of temporal power, though they thought it would be necessary to transform the papal government internally (above all by laicizing it broadly), and invoked the adherence of the pope as a temporal sovereign to the cause of Italian independence and federation.

Now, with the policies of Pius IX, all the obstacles seemed to be overcome within a few months. He took the path of liberal reforms, and with that seemed to be releasing the papacy from its ties to absolutism. He allowed the national sentiment of his subjects to express itself; and he himself seemed to show a feeling of Italianness when he uttered that famous sentence, "Oh, great God, bless Italy!" At least that was how it was understood throughout the peninsula. And so Pius IX was at once the Angelic Pope of the mystical and apocalyptic dreams of the Middle Ages, who was to bring about the renewal of the Church, and the pope of the *Primato*, which he was said to have carried with him into the conclave while he was still Cardinal Mastai-Ferretti. Gioberti was acclaimed "teacher of the pope," was considered a prophet, a new John the Baptist for the new Christ. There was partial laicization of the government, with the formation of a regular ministry; there was a discreet freedom of the press in law and even more in practice; there was a Council of State that hinted (despite the pope's protests) at a constitution; there was a Civic Guard, which meant the beginning of self-government and protection against the arbitrary action of the police. Above all, the people could demonstrate, agitate, become active, become the protagonist on the political scene, much more so than they had been at the time the revolution was brought to Italy from France. Metternich and Solaro della Margarita were quite rightly disturbed: initiative was passing from the government to the people.

3. From Reform to Revolution

From the Papal States, the movement spread to many parts of the peninsula, always with the tolerance of the governments. Through the calculated and organized work of the patriots, Tuscany became the first center for its propagation. The third place went to Piedmont, where there had been indications of awakening and royal change even before the election of Pius IX. There were important manifestations of this in the second half of 1846: the congress of the Agrarian Association at Mortara, the congress of Italian scientists at Genoa, and the celebration of the centenary of Balilla. Even Lombardy-Venetia, under the Austrian police, found a way to start agitating, behind the screen of religious enthusiasm for Pius IX or for the new archbishop of Milan, Romilli, who succeeded the Austrian Gaysruck. (So far as liberalism was concerned, Romilli might well have learned a thing or two from his predecessor.) There was a great upsurge of liberal-patriotic propaganda throughout Italy. Partly because of able direction behind the scenes, partly because of a spontaneous impulse and the sudden outburst of what had been a slow, manifold germination, that propaganda was able to utilize any circumstance, any occasion or pretext, for the mobilization of Italian spirits.

Resistance on the part of governments was not lacking. Pius IX tried repeatedly to put an end to the demonstrations of approval that were trying to drag him ever forward; but at the same time he liked those demonstrations, because of a certain personal vanity that was by no means a negligible factor in the situation. In Tuscany, the police moved on to expulsions, warnings, and the arrest of suspected persons. At first, Charles Albert stuck tenaciously to Solaro della Margarita and rejected the reforms to which the pope and the grand duke had acceded; but then, in October, 1847, he turned about and conceded many and broad reforms. The three reforming states approached each other; negotiations began for a customs union among Rome, Florence, and Turin, and news of it spread throughout Italy, raising enthusiasm and hopes. It was the sketch for an Italian confederation, and the entire reform program was about to be put to the test.

The final push came not from governmental initiative (as had been the case in the beginning, with the papal amnesty), but from a popular insurrection, the Sicilian revolution. In spirit and character, it was a typically local, indigenous revolution. Sicilian autonomy returned to the scene, in the form and scope it had assumed from 1812 on. But there were European elements in the Sicilian constitution of 1812, which the autonomists were asking for again. Above all, the Sicilian revolution became a national event through its repercussions in Naples. The initiative between the "two Sicilies" was reversed: the Sicilian insurrection promoted the Neapolitan uprising and the concession, on January 29, 1848, of a constitution from Ferdinand II. That did not cause Sicily to join with Naples any more than it had in 1820; in the name of its autonomy, Sicily even went so far as to proclaim the fall of the Bourbons.

With the proclamation of the constitution, Naples not only joined the three reforming states, but now suddenly jumped beyond them; and they were forced to follow. Even the pope had to find some way to combine theocracy with constitutional government. It was a national upheaval, from which only Lombardy-Venetia and the duchies were absent, because of the foreign force of Austria. The connection between the cause of independence and the cause of liberty appeared clear.

4. Italy and Europe

In less than two years, the politically most retrograde country in Central Western Europe had taken on an appearance similar to that of France, England, and Switzerland. This fact aroused great interest in Europe; now people began to have a concrete notion of the Italian national personality and a genuine feeling for the Italian national question as a European problem. One could even speak of a European initiative on the part of Italy—Mazzini's dream, though he was not satisfied with the form it had taken. He thought that the people were not adequately playing the role of protagonist in this movement, that they were showing too little dignity before the sovereigns. And he continued to oppose the compromise of a constitutional monarchy. Compared with France under Louis Philippe, ever more enclosed in its bourgeois oligarchy, Italy in early 1848, with its people agitating in the squares and its uncompromising affirmations of independence and liberty, might seem to be way ahead.

As a consequence of the conflict with England over the "Spanish marriages," France had now turned decidedly toward understanding with Austria. The Guizot-Metternich idyl was flourishing, and it appeared to be the logical outcome of a certain moderatism, worthy of the same liberal, if the etymology of *lucus* from *non lucendo* be accurate. In the Swiss conflict of the Sonderbund, the Franco-Austrian understanding opposed Swiss liberalism, which nevertheless triumphed in the civil war and in the federal constitution of 1848. In Italy, too, that understanding worked against the Italian reform movement; only nuances of attitude distinguished the aims of French from Austrian policy—remnants of modesty in the "citizen king," who had by this time gone over completely to conservatism, though to be sure he never thought of violating the constitution.

Opposed to France and Austria, who were proceeding arm in arm, there was England. England might have put up with an Austria antagonistic to Russia, but not with an Austro-Russian union in the Holy Alliance; and as for France, which was not only its Mediterranean rival but had now attached itself to the Austro-Russian entente, England could no longer have any sympathy at all. When Palmerston returned to the ministry of foreign affairs, just at the time of the election of Pius IX, he favored the liberal movements in all of Europe and particularly in Italy. A pacified and fortified Italy as a counter-balance to Austria and France seemed desirable to him. The idea of Italy as a nation useful to the equilibrium and peace of Europe, which Italian patriots had already formulated at the end of the Napeolonic period, now penetrated the inner re-cesses of diplomacy. Palmerston's policies reflected English public opinion, which had been worked on effectively by Mazzini. Then there was the mission of Lord Minto to Italy; Cobden, the apostle of free trade, also came, free of any offi-cial ties. He made a triumphal tour of Italy, and was celebrated even in Milan, with the tolerance of the Austrian authorities. As was logical, the economic free-trade movement was joining the political liberal movement. In this way, too, the European-ism of the very Italian revolution of 1848 was being con-secrated.

5. Italy and Austria

Despite the understanding with Guizot, Metternich tempo-rized while champing the bit. He knew that Austria was not very stable, that in fact it was already creaking; and he knew, too, that he was no longer master, as he had been at the time of Francis I. No one understood better than he that the Italian liberal-national movement threatened to lead to Lombard insurrection and to an Italian war against Austria. The move-ment was already deeply colored with anti-Austrianism. All this made an accord between the movement and Charles Albert much easier, for he had already assumed a resolute attitude against Austria at the beginning of 1846 because of certain customs questions. For no one was the change in papal policy as important as it was for Charles Albert. Religious to the point of asceticism and bigotry, it was only through neo-Guelph auspices that he could accede to the Italian national movement. The demonstrations for the centenary of Balilla took place not only in Liguria and in Piedmont, but in all of Italy, forgetting, naturally, that the king of Sardinia had been the ally of Austria when she was expelled from Genoa. Ripened national sentiment and reawakened national pride were directed against Austria. Neo-Guelphism evoked the battles of the popes against the German emperors, and of Alexander III allied to the Lombard League. The history of the Lombard League, written by the Monte Cassino monk Tosti, who was the incarnation of neo-Guelphism, was announced right on the eve of the Lombard war. Agitation in Lombardy-Venetia became even more intense; just then, Correnti's *L'Austria e la Lombardia* was published, and enjoyed great success in clandestine circulation. Aside from the demonstrations and the conflicts, there was the beginning of a legal resistance (following Cattaneo's ideas); and that was particularly effective toward a government that, although absolutistic and police-ridden, was nevertheless legalistic, and would not very easily have recourse to purely arbitrary violence.

Perhaps even at this point, if Austria had pursued a more flexible and more intelligent policy than that of the doctrinaire and by now calcified Metternich, the blow might have been deflected through clever concessions. This is all the more true in that the Italian revolution—for such it must now be called—contained varied tendencies, attitudes, and possibilities so far as Austria was concerned. Certainly the militant current was not lacking, and the contacts of 1821 between Lombardy and Piedmont were now re-established. The Austro-Papal conflict over the occupation of the city of Ferrara in the summer of 1847 had had repercussions in all of Italy, and had made Charles Albert's heart jump. But by December there had been a diplomatic settlement; both sides temporized, fearing a strong solution. Having taken the road of internal transformation ever more decidedly, the Italian revolution contained within it something that held it back from foreign military complications. Improvised constitutional Italy felt the need to consolidate and work itself out practically; moreover, the federative beginnings still had to take shape. Ferrari deprecated a clash with Austria because it risked arresting the liberal-reform movement, which of necessity would not be favored by a war. Cattaneo was still thinking of an evolution within a federal Austria; his liberal radicalism also favored a non-military solution. The decisive push toward war came from abroad.

6. *The European Revolution*

Although the Italian revolution had found sympathy in European liberal circles and had also been of interest to European diplomacy (bringing greatly increased prestige and importance to our country), it was not capable of revolutionizing Europe completely on its own. Given its moderate-Guelph character, it did contribute something toward reconciling conservative Catholic circles with the new ideas. It was, that is to say, one of the most conspicuous forms of liberal Catholicism in Europe. The results of that reconciliation were visible in France, when the February revolution toppled the throne of Louis Philippe. Neither the clergy nor the upper classes rose to support him or to regret his end. The popular republic was accepted unanimously, and the adherence of the clergy was particularly quick and clamorous. There was a clerical-republican idyl, in an atmosphere reminiscent of the Middle Ages.

Unlike the Italian revolution, the French revolution spread immediately throughout Europe. Once again, the European initiative (contrary to Mazzini's sympathies and hopes) came from France. The French revolution gave birth to the German revolution, both in Vienna and in Berlin. A new fact of capital importance was that the Austrian problem was now posed in all its breadth: the problem, that is, of the diverse peoples joined under the Hapsburg scepter. Mazzini's idea seemed to triumph, even though it was not through Italian initiative. For some time, he had viewed Italian liberation from Austria as part of a general liberation of the peoples under Austria, and as part of the dissolution of the Hapsburg Empire. In this, too, he was in disagreement with the Italian moderates, who considered the cause of Italian independence separate. In fact, they favored a peaceful solution (Balbo) that sought not only the preservation but the expansion of Austria in the direction of the Balkans. On this score, Cattaneo stood with the moderates (cf. above, p. 104): federalism was being transported from Italy to the Danube. In Austria itself, many of the reawakened peoples were also moving in the direction of federalism. The Czech apostle Palácky coined the phrase that if Austria had not existed, it would have been necessary to invent her. Opposed to federalism, there was Mazzini's idea of national unity. To be sure, he wanted a European federation, but only after the integral recomposition of each nationality. He did not ask himself whether that was anthropogeographically possible, or whether the national exasperation caused by struggle and union, based on a different program for each nation, was the best moral preparation for the desired federation of the peoples.

7. Piedmontese Intervention and Defeat, and the Failure of Federalism

For Italy, the outbreak of the Austrian revolution put an end to the hesitation between a peaceful or military solution, and to any doubts whether Lombardy-Venetia ought to be federally included within the Empire or separated from it. Once the various peoples subject to Austria had arisen, the Lombard-Venetians had no choice but to try somehow to join the rest of Italy. The problem of "federalism or unity" was now posed only within the Italian borders.

When the insurrection of the Five Days broke out, even

Cattaneo immediately understood the new situation and became an enlightened and intrepid leader of the people in arms. Where would the movement end? The majority of the combatants did not think beyond their immediate task, the expulsion of Austria. Some, especially in the upper classes, had thought of union with Piedmont even before the insurrection. Cattaneo—and not only he—wanted a Lombard republic. But that had no tradition, or at best a Milanese tradition, and even that was cut off by the many centuries since the early Middle Ages. The case of Venice was different, for there the proclamation of the Republic of Saint Mark was an obvious step: a good number of living Venetians had been born under it. But in Venice, too, the resurrection of the past could not resolve the problem of relations with the rest of Venetia, for these could no longer be relations of lords to subjects. In Lombardy, there was an analogous problem between Milan and the provinces. But the main complication came from without, with the intervention of Piedmont.

Urged by some of the Milanese, Charles Albert stopped hesitating (though not before Milan had liberated itself) and took the field against the Austrian army, which was retreating toward the Quadrilateral. He proclaimed he was coming to bring the help of one brother to another; the adoption of the tricolor with the Savoyard cross on it was the symbol of royal adherence to the Italian cause. Charles Albert was sincere when he said he was entering the lists as the champion of Italian independence; but that was not his only motive. There were two others, at least as powerful. The king was thinking about the traditional Savoyard program for the annexation of Lombardy. (He may also have recalled the opinion expressed by Galeani Napione at the end of the eighteenth century that it was better for Savoy to have Lombardy belong to another state than to have it be autonomous.) Aside from this territorial desire, there was the fear of a republic, which was just what an independent Lombardy would very probably become. Standing between the two fires of a probable Lombard republic and an already existing French republic, Charles Albert feared he would be surrounded and destroyed. The justification used by his government before the great monarchical powers for his intervention in Lombardy—namely, the necessity for forestalling the republican danger—was anything but a pretext. That justification was sent even to Austria, instead of a declaration of war. Before the eyes of Europe, Charles Albert, at the very moment he was starting a war of independence, was hiding the light of the national idea under the bushel of monarchical conservatism.

The federal republicans (among them Giuseppe Ferrari, who came from France to Milan temporarily) were decidedly against the monarchical-Savoyard initiative for the twin reasons of liberty and federation. In February, 1848, Cattaneo had told the Piedmontese to make their own revolution at home first, and not to come "with your courts and your confessionals, to make us fall even lower than turtles." Mazzini, on the other hand, adjusted to the Piedmontese intervention. He accepted Charles Albert's motto *l'Italia farà da sè*; that is to say, like the king, he opposed French intervention. Anticipating his attitude of 1860, he declared himself disposed to support the king fully, provided he set about to realize the unity of Italy. By that time, Mazzini had already come to consider unity more important than the republic, and he rightly saw the intrinsic opposition between Savoyard intervention and the federalist movement, an opposition that was still not clear to many. (Charles Albert himself would have fled from the idea of dethroning the pope.) In fact, it was not only republican federalism that was shaken to the roots by the Piedmontese intervention, but monarchical federalism as well. If Piedmont won the war, it would get Lombardy and Venetia, as well as the duchies. Master of all Northern Italy, Piedmont would have hegemony throughout the peninsula. What would the other states do, particularly the

Kingdom of Naples, the other great state? The only course open to Naples would be to pounce on the papal territories; but the legitimism and, even more, the clericalism of Ferdinand II ruled that out. Other attitudes on the part of Piedmont (especially its lukewarmness toward the idea of a league) could only confirm the suspicions of Italian princes concerning Piedmontese aspirations.

The only solution to the federal crisis would have been for Venetia to join the Republic of Saint Mark, for Lombardy to make itself a republic, and for both to put strong forces in the field, so that they might appear to be allies, and not vassals of Piedmont. But republics and republican armies would certainly not be welcomed by Charles Albert or any other monarch. A great question for the historiography of 1848 concerns the inadequate organization and action of the volunteers against Austria; but there seems little doubt that the principal causes of that inadequacy were the hostility of Piedmont and the lack of interest of the Lombard moderates or fusionists. They had to ask themselves whether Piedmont-Savoy would have continued to fight if a Lombard republic were proclaimed, and if so, how energetically? Surely the negative answer to this question must have played a leading role in the resounding success of the annexationist party in Milan, apart from all the conservative interests that contributed to it. Aside from any question of how it was done, the holding of a plebiscite broke an earlier pledge to put off all decisions to the end of the war. Moreover, the plebiscite was held under very forced circumstances: in the eyes of the multitude, the choice was not between annexation to Piedmont or an autonomous state, but between Piedmontese defense against Austria or isolation. The fact that the plebiscite in favor of union stipulated as a condition the formation of a constituent assembly—a condition which later gave rise to many controversies in Piedmont—did nothing to change the main point, for the preservation of the Savoyard constitutional monarchy had already been determined beforehand.

The failure of federalism and the triumph of Piedmontese annexationism had very important consequences. The incipient association of the Italian princes among themselves and against Austria was dissolved; the truce among the parties was ended. (Judging that the pledge had been broken, Mazzini raised the banner of republicanism in Milan, though he refrained from revolutionary action.) A battle was unleashed, embittered by mutual suspicions and accusations, little less than a "war of all against all." (Gioberti later gave an account of it in his *Rinnovamento*, with grandiosity of line and incisiveness of art, but not without distortion of reality.) So far as the war of independence was concerned, it became more a royal-Piedmontese than a national-popular enterprise. Promoting and imposing plebiscites from Milan to Venice, Charles Albert was now saying, "I take it upon myself." It was no longer *l'Italia farà da sè*, but *Piemonte farà da sè*.

It soon became clear that the load was more than those shoulders could bear. This is not the place to give an analysis of the Piedmontese military campaigns of 1848–49. What is incontestable is that Piedmont was militarily unprepared—a proof, aside from others, that there is no basis for interpreting the policies of Charles Albert in the fifteen-year period of absolutism as a preparation for the war. Even worse was the lack of moral preparation—in fact, there was the very opposite of moral preparation. The entire royal-governmental inspiration during that fifteen-year period had come from the Holy Alliance and understanding with Austria. For those who had been educated in this atmosphere, how could Austria suddenly become the mortal enemy? The war was carried on by high Piedmontese officialdom as a duty of office, out of dynastic loyalty much more than national sentiment. High Piedmontese personalities (even Charles Albert himself) testify that the army was surprised at "the sudden irruption" against Austria, and was anything but enthusiastic about the Italian cause. The substitution of the tricolor (hitherto the flag of revolution) for the ancient flag of Savoy aroused an unpleasant sense in officialdom. The duke of Genoa, brother of Victor Emmanuel, tells us in his final report on the war that officers and soldiers went forth to fight for a cause completely contrary to the principles by which they had been raised. The moral conditions that produce heroic tenacity cannot be improvised; minds cannot be moved right and left, back and forth, to the beat of the government's baton. It must be added that the Italian peninsula produced no sweeping movement of martial volunteers eager to throw out the foreigner; but we must ask whether such movements can take place when there is no decisive push from the governments or the ruling classes, or when there is no real revolution to remove the one as well as the other, as was the case in the France of the First Republic.

The failure to pursue Radetzky's army in its difficult retreat from Milan, the even more important failure to envelop and conquer the Quadrilateral, and the failure to take up positions at the Alpine passes were of capital importance for the unhappy end of the war. As a result of those failures, the tactics used at the Quadrilateral were defenseive, passive, and inert; moreover, Venetia had to be abandoned. These military blunders were also grave political errors, and led to suspicion of treachery: Charles Albert, it was phantasied, had failed to crush the Austrian army and assure the freedom of Venetia because he wanted to have an easier time getting Lombardy through negotiations with the powers. The king's acceptance of the idea of treating with Austria through Franco-English mediation—behind which there really was his inclination to be satisfied with the Adige as a border—seemed to confirm these suspicions. With mediation, the popular war would be abandoned in favor of diplomacy; the Italian problem, to be sure, would become European, but it would be back in the hands of governments, not of the peoples. The capitulation of Milan immediately after the promise to defend it to the bitter end (a promise made, it seems, when the retreat had already been planned) encouraged further cries of treachery. But there was no treachery; there were only grave insufficiencies and inconsistencies reflecting the various and often contradictory interests that had influenced the conduct of the war. Even the cause of the unhappy retreat to Milan was probably just worry over a republican pronouncement in the Lombard capital threatening the Savoyard rights derived from the plebiscite.

8. The Incomplete Revolutionary Crisis

In the other states that withdrew from the national war (volunteers after all did not bind their governments), internal crises broke out: moderate liberals against democrats, monarchists against republicans, federalists against unitarians. The brilliant union of governments and peoples fell apart as soon as the former showed they were not going to be compliant to the pressures of the latter; moreover, the people could not agree on the direction in which pressure was to be applied. So far as the governments were concerned, it was part irresolution and part bad will, in different proportions in the different states. Bad will was greatest in Naples: there seems to be no doubt that the Bourbon planned to take the first occasion (which came on May 15) to arrest the liberal movement and become master once again by setting aside and liquidating the constitution. All the paladins of Bourbonism cannot change this diagnosis. As soon as it could, the Lazzaronian bigotry of Ferdinand II poured forth in its natural direction. In Tuscany, there was ineptitude without premeditated ill will on the part of the grand duke and the moderates. There was also the long-winded confusion of parties and prominent men, and a pitiful alternation of governments, each of them incapable of directing public opinion. The much-berated Guerrazzi did no worse than his moderate vituperators. Then there was the flight of the grand duke (here duplicity began to join ineptitude), the vague proclamation of a constituent assembly, and the moderates' *coup d'état* on behalf of the grand duke. They failed to see that instead of avoiding Austria, they were throwing themselves into her clutches.

More calamitous, and for that very reason more instructive, was the way things went in the Papal States. There were two antitheses there: one between the universal religious head and the Italian prince, and the other between theocracy and a liberal constitution. The first led to the crisis of April 29, palliated (but no more) by putting Durando's army behind Charles Albert. The second unfolded in a series of ministerial crises, and led to the assassination of Pellegrino Rossi, the flight of the pope, the constituent assembly, and the republic. The Roman constituent assembly was the only realization of the idea of self-determination of the people, which had been propounded on so many sides and in so many ways; the highest affirmation of national sovereignty took place in Rome. The flight of Pius IX and his behavior at Gaeta constituted a moral abdication and worse; but the normal political consequences of such a move were forestalled by the sacred claims of legitimacy, according to which the people were required to wait passively for the decisions of the pope and for those who executed them. The citizens were expected to refrain from speaking through their constituent assembly, even in favor of the pope—a claim to which the moderates, or at least the most conspicuous part of them, submitted by abstaining. The pope expected the restitution of the "sacred deposit" not from the people but by theocratic right, which in practice meant by foreign arms. It was to foreign arms that Pius IX entrusted his cause, thus continuing that series of papal appeals for the invasion of Italy that went from the appeal of Pope Stephen to Pepin to that of Julius II to the Swiss. This marked the definite divorce between Italy and the temporal papacy. The fall of temporal power does not date from September 20, 1870, but from February 9, 1849.

Piedmont also experienced its own internal political crisis, but it was less grave. There was some timid parliamentary constitutionalism on the part of the moderates, amidst the first fears of socialism (events in France lent importance to these Italian socialist activities, which were more numerous than is generally believed, though all in all of little importance); and there were the verbal assertions of the democrats, to which Gioberti temporarily and hesitatingly acceded. The monarchical constitutional assembly did not have time to become a reality, since it was rendered pointless by the Austrian reconquest of Lombardy. The resumption of the war of independence alleviated internal troubles (which was why Cavour favored it), for it neutralized the democratic opposition, which had become the main proponent of the war.

9. *Testimony of Blood*

The events of 1848 came to an end with three military episodes: Novara, Rome, and Venice. From a purely military point of view, the first was rather shabby, and even less than shabby. Ineptitude and defeatism vied with each other, with the latter perhaps prevailing. Still, now that Austria had consolidated herself and Piedmont stood alone in Italy and Europe, this almost desperate initiative had some moral value. Herein lay the greatness of Charles Albert's undertaking, which ended with his sacrifice of the crown (about which he had been thinking even in case of victory) and with his silent exile. And just as one poet of the Risorgimento used his pen to revile Charles Albert at the time of his greatest humiliation, so another and greater poet of the post-Risorgimento depicted his final exaltation, showing him brought before God by the martyrs for the fatherland, who now counted him among their number.

Rome, which entered the Risorgimento with the agitations of 1846–47, rose to the heights of it with the defense of 1849. And with Rome rose all of Italy, for Italians came from all parts to fight against the foreigner, the servant and accomplice of European reaction. The depths of a war of domination, plunder, and oppression are equaled by the heights attained when life is sacrificed in supreme testimony of a cause that has moral value. Such was the sacrifice of the defenders of Rome in the last desperate battles of June, 1849; they knew their victory could lie only in death against an enemy who was materially certain to overpower them. But their intention was precisely to testify with their lives to the reality of the Italian nation. And the same value of testimonial martyrdom lay in the defense of Venice, which was almost more desperate than that of Rome, because there was not even a minimal hope of any change in the policies of the enemy. Abandoned to themselves, Rome and Venice consecrated Italian independence and liberty before the world, defending them in the tradition of the medieval citizen communes, with the spirit of the modern religion of liberty, and with that faith in the ideal that persists and triumphs over barbarian insolence, provided it finds people ready to die for it.

10. *Diagnosis of 1848*

Gioberti's last book, *Del Rinnovamento civile d'Italia*, was superior to the *Primato*, inasmuch as historical-political speculation prevailed over propaganda, pettifogging, and sacerdotal eloquence. Gioberti contrasted the Risorgimento, the events of 1848 that had recently taken place and failed, with the Rinnovamento, the future process by which Italy would really be resuscitated. The former, he says, had an indigenous character, an evolutionary course, and a federal program; the latter would be European, revolutionary, and unitarian. The diagnosis and prognosis are traced with great sagacity, and are expressed in a much more concise and robust style than the *Primato*. From the very beginning, the Giobertian conception of the two periods was accepted by what might be called second-rate and semiofficial national historiography (although the two different terms were not accepted, and the name Risorgimento remained common to both periods). Since the French alliance and unity under the Savoyard monarchy were the two basic features of the concluding period of the Risorgimento, there was a perfect correspondence to the Giobertian prognosis, which acquired the undisputed fame of a prophecy. Several years ago, one of the most able scholars of the Risorgimento re-examined the character and success of the Giobertian prophecy. He came to conclusions notably different from the common ones, and he was right.

We shall say something of this later. Right now, before looking at the prognosis of the *Rinnovamento*, we should like to examine the diagnosis of the Risorgimento. Gioberti presented the events of 1846–48 in the light of his *Primato*, which was natural enough (especially from someone who was such a capable and sometimes even sophistical advocate of his own infallibility). From there, he got the resolute affirmation of the indigenous, evolutionary-conservative, federal character of the movement. With that, Gioberti was insisting on the point of departure and neglecting the point of arrival; or, rather, he was considering the point of arrival a deviation, a degeneration of the original movement. Such a consideration was rather obvious, since the point of arrival was a palpable failure. But one must look into that failure to decide whether it was really due to a degenerative process, or whether there was not an inner logic in what he calls degeneration, whether there were not real needs, and if there were, to see whether they were met later. Indeed, if we accept the meaning given to those events in the Giobertian terminology, we might well find ourselves asking whether we ought not at least partially to reverse the positions and call the events up to 1848 the Rinnovamento.

The reform movement of 1846–48, as we have seen, had popular initiative behind it; the pressure of the people produced it. If its content was moderate, the manner of carrying it out (which counts a great deal in politics) can be called semi-revolutionary. A single, completely spontaneous governmental act preceded that popular initiative and pressure: the amnesty of Pius IX. And even that act acquired its extraordinary propulsive force only because it came at a time when the national situation had already been prepared—and not by the governments. The decisive phase of the reforms, which was the constitutional phase, came after the Sicilian revolution (which was a true and genuine revolution, even formally). Then came the war of independence, which was no longer a matter of reform or evolution, but of revolution; for war, which is the opposite of a peaceful evolution or compromise, is by its very nature revolutionary. That is even more true of a war of principles, such as the Italian war of independence against Austrian legitimist monarchy and the treaties of Vienna. We saw how the war interfered with the evolutionary-confederative process, changing and deviating it. Furthermore, this war was nothing but a consequence of the Five Days—that is to say, of the Lombard-Venetian revolution—which in turn was a repercussion of the French revolution and part of the European revolution unleashed by it. With that, the purely indigenous character of 1848 disappears; nor can one speak of misled individuals or of a degenerative process. What we have is an iron concatenation of events superior to any individual initiative, and corresponding to the spirit, the logic, and the ideal needs of the Risorgimento itself.

The first phase of 1848 does not, then, have the purely evolutionary character Gioberti said it did; nor can the fact of revolution be represented as a brusque reversal, or as an arbitrary alteration of the initial process. In the *Rinnovamento*, Gioberti speaks bitterly of the "puritans," those intransigent republicans, those republicans of principle. There is no need to bring up here his unjust, even outrageous, judgment of Mazzini, for it belongs to ephemeral politics. The point is whether the republican program of 1848–49 was really a priori dogmatism, a form of premeditated, factious, and ruinous intrusion. We already saw that such was not the case. The major cause of the failure was the dearth and the defection of princes, which Gioberti himself recognized, not without some self-contradiction. The failure was also due to the incapacity of moderatism to organize and direct the movement after having pushed it into the town squares, and to its unwillingness to pose the republican question. Except for Piedmont, all the governments failed in the internal task of installing a new liberal and popular order (the autonomous Sicilian monarchy lacked a sovereign when the duke of Genoa refused the crown); and all except Piedmont withdrew from the external task, the war of independence against Austria. Finally: Piedmont failed twice in the task it took on. The reduction of the national-popular war to a royal-Savoyard war did not prove fortunate.

Under such conditions, a completely logical development of the national revolution would have required aiming at the fall of all the governments and at the establishment of republican democracies, united against Austria and the sovereigns. The only question then would be whether the unitarian program of Mazzini or the federalist program of the radicals would triumph. (While he was master in Rome, Mazzini was in fact disposed to accept federation even with monarchical Piedmont.) Aside from the Roman and the Venetian republics, there were republican beginnings in Tuscany, and even in the Piedmontese state, with the insurrection in Genoa.

Since foreign intervention suffocated the experiment, it is impossible to pronounce a definite judgment. But notice that the democratic leaders, even the most determined, idealistic, and dogmatic, posed the question of the republic not as an a priori dictatorial imposition, but on the basis of an appeal to the people through the constituent assembly. The constituent assemblies—or the Italian constituent assembly (of which the Roman Assembly considered itself the first session) —were nothing but the natural outcome of the national movement. The Italian people, now conscious of themselves, were clearly posing the problem of their destinies; abandoned by false, fleeing princes, they were getting ready to solve the problem through self-determination. It is quite true that there was immaturity and inexperience in the movement, and that the masses were as yet little affected by national consciousness. But a state of urgent necessity prevailed, and no demagogue had deliberately created it, as Gioberti liked to suppose. Moreover, there is no revolution that does not bear those negative characteristics. If political action required waiting for the full maturity of the people, or even only of the so-called leading classes, there would never be any political action. History would petrify the status quo into immobility.

11. *The People's International* MANQUÉ

There was true revolution, then, in 1848. In fact, it was the truest national revolution of the Risorgimento, the only one that arrived (at least in one of its episodes) at complete expression; i.e., at full self-determination of the people. This revolution was not a degeneration, but a logical development whose failure had lasting consequences. Indeed, we may well ask whether the rupture it caused in the national-popular course of the Risorgimento has ever healed completely. It is true that there is a difference between the first period of the Risorgimento, which ended in the catastrophe of 1849, and the second period, which realized unity. But of the two periods, the first was more truly revolutionary, whereas the second saw evolution and compromise not only in Italian but in European affairs as well. For it was not just the history of Italy (and this is a fundamental point to which we shall return) that took a different tack after 1848, but the history of all Europe.

Perhaps the greatest lacuna in Gioberti's criticism of 1848 is that he does not at all consider its international aspect, whereas he does give a clearly international framework to the succeeding period. Here again, he starts out with his "category" of the indigenous Risorgimento. The beginnings and the development of the events of 1848 were indeed clearly national, up to and including the Sicilian revolution; but the double revolutionary explosion against Austria and the indigenous princes came after the European revolution and was caused by it. The twenty-fifth of February in Paris produced the thirteenth of March in Vienna, and that in turn unleashed the Five Days. The French republic had its influence on republican movements and accomplishments in Venice, Milan, Florence, Genoa, and Rome, even if that influence was not as direct as one might suppose by looking at things on the whole and from a distance. The February republic had a moderate character, idyllic toward the inside, and conservative, timid toward the outside. It renounced European propaganda; it was almost a re-edition of the July Monarchy in the "resistance" phase. That represented a fundamental—in fact, fatal—weakness for European developments, retarding them by a century and rendering them far more laborious, complicated, bloody, and destructive. There were, to be sure, the socialist agitations, up to the revolutionary outburst of June, 1848, but they were quickly and decisively crushed. It was not Louis Napoleon but Cavaignac who dealt the mortal blow to the revolution, imagining that he was saving liberty. June 13, 1849, was a last-ditch effort; by then, the revolution in all Europe was extinguished.

Just as 1848 is the true national Italian revolution, it is also the true European international revolution. (The revolution of 1789 was a *French* revolution, with European repercussions and Franco-revolutionary occupations and dictatorships in various parts of Europe.) Though the upheaval began in France, the uprisings of 1848 took place almost at the same time in a large part of Europe. If the spark was French, each country had gone through the ideal and practical long-range preparation on its own, though at the same time in contact with the other countries. It is reasonable to think that if the revolution had consolidated itself in France, Germany, Austria, and Italy, its effects would also have been felt in Spain, the Balkans, and Scandinavia; Switzerland, in fact, was transformed from a *Staatenbund* to a *Bundesstaat* precisely in 1848; and there were minor repercussions in other countries, of which we need not speak here. And yet an upheaval so vast and so profound failed. What is the reason? The usual talk about immaturity and excesses explains nothing; it is too general, and it points out phenomena that are just as common to successful as to unsuccessful revolutions. It is nothing but moralistic or paternalistic whining by little moderates. We must get to more concrete explanations. These seem reducible to two: the clash of socialism and liberalism, and of democracy and nationalism. The first was of decisive importance in France, and the second in the rest of Europe; but the second also had influence on the French failure, just as the first did on the European failures.

The red flag raised in 1848 as the symbol of the proletariat and the social republic frightened and disgusted the bourgeoisie, both liberal and conservative. The "red peril" set the bourgeoisie against the proletariat, neatly dividing the liberal-democratic following in two, and pushing the bourgeois part back to the point of reaction and dictatorship. Even at a distance of almost a century, we are deeply impressed by the spectacle of Montalembert and—more important—Cavour trembling with fear or livid with hatred when confronted with danger to the "social order"; and to avert that danger, they are ready to bend their sabers and kiss the aspergillum. Only after socialism was crushed in France did Cavour continue his liberal evolution. What effect the fear of socialism had on Cavour has not been adequately studied, and its effect on the entire liberal movement of 1848 is even less well known. We also have no adequate study of the Italian socialist movements in that period. On the whole, it would seem that fear of socialism did not have the primary importance in Italy in 1848 that it undoubtedly had in France (for the simple reason that the "red peril" was not as strong in Italy). In France, it generated the conservative majority in the Legislative Assembly, the presidency of Louis Napoleon, and the *coup d'état*. Ever since then, whenever the bourgeoisie in Europe found themselves placed between loss of freedom and fear for their pocketbooks, they have (when the fear reached a certain level) been inclined to pay more attention to the latter, without asking whether, in the final analysis, they were not thus piling the two dangers together.

On the European level, the other factor in the failure of 1848 seems more decisive. The various nations that had arisen did not come to any agreement among themselves, as Mazzini had piously presupposed. Some (like France), secure in their own ancient existence, remained aside to observe the battles of the younger nations. (Diplomatic intervention and hints at military intervention did nothing to change this fact, both because they were inconclusive and because they remained on the level of the old politics.) They did not understand that their own internal liberty and their own future in Europe depended on the outcome of this battle. The young nationalities not only did not help each other but disagreed and fought with each other. German nationalists fought against Slavs and Italians; our people tried in vain to get the Frankfurt Assembly to recognize the Trentino as Italian. Marshal Radetzky, the restorer of Austrian dominion in Italy (and its hangman a few years later), figured as a national German hero. The Hungarians behaved no better toward the Croatians; and these in turn furnished the Hapsburg emperor with his most bellicose battalions against Hungary. The solidarity of the peoples against the common oppressor was almost totally lacking. There was some diplomatic contact between Italy and Hungary, some desire on the part of Italians (Gioberti, Cavour, and of course Mazzini) for an understanding with the Slavs and the Rumanians, but that did nothing to change the state of things. There was, instead, solidarity in the opposite camp: the Czar had the Russian army march against the Hungarians, making possible the hangings at Arad; while young Bismarck applauded, the king of Prussia preferred—"royally," Giusti would have said—the humiliation of Olmütz under the Austrian and Russian rod to the role of head of the free German nationality. On June 13, 1849, the last Parisian democratic insurrection failed; June 18 saw the dispersal of the German constituent assembly by the police of Stuttgart; on July 4, Rome fell before the attack of Louis Napoleon's troops; on August 13, the Hungarians capitulated at Vilagos; on the twenty-third, Venice capitulated. The coalition of the peoples had failed to come about; the coalition of the governments had won.

It was not a final victory. The solidarity of the governments was soon shaken by the policies of Napoleon III. But a moment like 1848, a moment of joint effort by the people for liberation and federation, was never to return. The ideal of Mazzini and Cattaneo remained unrealized. And the prophecy of Gioberti in the *Rinnovamento*, that the European democratic movement would generate and include the Italian Rinnovamento, did not come true, at least not in that direct and integral form.

CHAPTER VI

Unification

1. The New Piedmont

Revocation of the constitutions was a logical development in the reaction of the Italian governments to 1848, as were foreign intervention and occupation (Austria in the Legations, the duchies, and Tuscany, and France in Rome). The final republican development had not taken place, and monarchical-constitutional federalism had disappeared. The failure of the second appeared more complete than the first, which could at least boast the defense of Rome and Venice. Monarchical federalism as a possible solution to the Italian problem was eliminated, although there were some who did not know it, and made attempts to continue it (even on an international scale). Together with monarchical federalism, the neo-Guelph conception of the Risorgimento received a death blow: the illusion of a national papacy, or of a pope leading the nation, had been dispelled. This was an important point in favor of liberal Europeanism in the course of the Risorgimento, for it meant the elimination of one of the principal indigenous forces that pre-eminently represented the conservative and authoritarian traditions.

If Piedmont had passed into the reactionary camp (as it nearly did, for the ruling classes and the king seemed to be in favor of it), the democratic-republican solution, the solution of popular initiative pure and simple, though temporarily beaten by superior enemy forces, would have remained the only one in the field. Piedmont would have had to renounce its policy of Italian expansion and return to the policy of "artichoke leaves"; i.e., of limited, occasional expansion (taking the duchies, for example, or part of them). That was the policy favored by Solaro della Margarita; and it is the way some people view the Italian Risorgimento even today. But because Piedmont was the only state to keep its constitution, it could appear to be the champion of the new Italy even after the second Austrian victory. After all the other states had renounced the nation and the future by embracing reaction and the foreigner (which were indissolubly conjoined), Piedmont maintained its candidacy; and it did so by pursuing liberal domestic policies. Piedmont was following the suggestions of Cattaneo (cf. above, p. 104); it accepted the radical thesis of domestic reforms before independence. Even Balbo now recognized the necessity of proceeding that way.

The program for the new Piedmontese policies (which really were revolutionary compared to those of Charles Albert) was formulated by the *Rinnovamento* of Gioberti. Piedmont had to put an end to its "municipalism"; that meant the Piedmontese had to stop thinking of the destiny of their country as something apart from the destiny of Italy, and they had to stop seeing in Italy only an occasion for the aggrandizement of the Savoyard state. The war of independence itself had been afflicted with "municipalism," Gioberti said; and it was also the reason for the lack of accord with the other Italian states and peoples. Piedmont had to espouse the Italian cause frankly and totally. It could play a leading hegemonical role in the development of that cause so long as the final aim was the absorption of Piedmont by Italy, and not the opposite. The Savoyard monarchy would have to deal resolutely with the three modern problems: intellectual progress, nationality, and raising the status of the common people. "The Sardinian monarchy has hitherto been aristocratic, municipal, and un-receptive to talent; now it must become as progressive, demo-cratic, and national as possible." In other words, before taking on the leadership of Italy, Piedmont had to transform itself: precisely what Cattaneo (we must repeat it) had asked Pied-mont to do on the eve of the war of independence.

To Gioberti, then, the course of Piedmontese hegemony in Italy appeared not as the continuation of age-old policies, but as a reversal in the direction of the new European ideas. Modern Piedmont, said Gioberti, represents the principle of liberty in antithesis to Austria and the other Italian states; and the principle had to embody itself in civil reforms. The Siccardi law was a "distant prelude"; but Gioberti thought the path was not being followed with enough alacrity. As we know, he tied Italy's future chances to a democratic upheaval in Europe, promoted by France. The French republic would respect its ally, the Savoyard Kingdom; nevertheless, it was to be foreseen that all Europe would become republican, and the popular monarchy in Italy would have served as a stepping stone. Prophecies such as these from a historian-philosopher like Gioberti, or from a religious apostle like Mazzini, must be considered general long-range perspectives. Whatever else may be said, Gioberti was mistaken in forecasting an alliance of the French republic with the monarchy of Savoy; but he was not wrong in giving a primary place to the Franco-Sardinian alliance—or, rather, to the French government's assumption of the Italian cause. What mitigates the mistake in Gioberti's forecast (without eliminating it) is the fact that Napoleon III, at least to a certain degree, played the role that the republic of 1848 either could not or would not play in Europe.

2. *Victor Emmanuel II and Cavour*

At the end of his forecasts concerning Italy and Piedmont, Gioberti said he hardly dared to hope that Piedmontese hegemony would be realized, for there were so many obstacles to it within Piedmont itself. His only hope lay in the young king, who would have to give a personal direction to the policies of his government. We know from contemporary sources that Victor Emmanuel read the *Rinnovamento* with great attention; that alone seemed an important fact, for he was not in the habit of reading books. It must have made a great impression on him—one of those impressions we get when we see that others have given clear expression to ideas which we have glimpsed in a confused way, or which were dozing in the recesses of our subconscious. The personality of Victor Emmanuel has not yet been studied sufficiently; the effort necessary to penetrate his "secret" has not been made, partly because of the scarcity of intimate documents. According to a little-known anecdote, he was called "the last of the conquerors"; and though that designation may at first sound strange, as it did to the man who heard and reported it, it may well have hit the mark and hit it deeply. A basic intuition must have guided the sovereign, an intuition that was ingrained in his temperament and explains his personal action. He understood perhaps more clearly than any other leading Piedmontese personality that the only choices he had were to ascend to become king of Italy or descend to become "milord Savoy." (That much he saw even more clearly than Cavour—at least the Cavour of the first premiership.) That was precisely the Giobertian thesis. He would put himself at the head of the national movement, to direct, promote, and control it, so that the outcome would be monarchical and not republican; with one blow, or almost, he would transform the little Savoyard Kingdom into one of the great European powers. That was his plan of action.

From the start, the political-territorial program as a function of dynastic interests and political power was uppermost in the mind of Victor Emmanuel; Cavour, on the other hand, seemed to be dominated, at least until the Congress of Paris, by domestic political concerns, especially Piedmont's liberal-constitutional development as an autonomous state. In the *Rinnovamento*, Gioberti gives a particularly acute judgment of Cavour, who was then only a minister: on the one hand, he accuses him of municipal tendencies; on the other, he appreciates the fact that the Piedmontese municipalism of Cavour has a European physiognomy, inasmuch as he wants to bring Piedmont, alone, to the level of a great power. An excellent enterprise, but one which Gioberti did not think would succeed. Gioberti intuited a large part of Cavour's psychology, which up to that time was wont to move from Piedmont to Europe and from Europe to Italy, rather than from Piedmont directly to Italy. That psychology brought him close to the mental make-up of the republican federalists, despite the differences in their political theories and goals. For Cavour, as for them, the essential requirement was the development of liberty and of modern civilization within a single state. Cavour advocated this demand as a moderate, not as a radical; but his feelings about domestic reforms were much stronger than those of the moderates of 1848. The moderates sincerely considered reforms important, but they valued them largely as instruments or opportunities, whereas Cavour, between 1850 and 1855, looked upon liberty and the constitution as primary and intrinsic values: they were worth conquering and developing in and for themselves, even if they were to remain confined within the borders of Piedmont. For Cavour, the supreme need was free political activity, as a necessary achievement of civilization, and as a joyous expansion of the personality—above all, naturally, his own. In fact, so far as personality was concerned, Cavour felt something, even in the early days, that went beyond moderatism. In parliament, that something expressed itself through the *connubio*, which was so irksome to authentic moderates like Azeglio. Later, Cavour went beyond moderatism on the national political level through his alliance with the revolution, from which he accepted the principle of the deposition and proclamation of kings by popular vote.

3. *The Politics of the* CONNUBIO

The policy of the new Piedmont was carried out first of all
in confessional affairs. The Siccardi law, calling for the abolition of ecclesiastical courts, was passed with Cavour taking a
leading part, though he was not yet a minister. It was an
application of liberal policies, and a realization of equality
before the law; it was also a logical consequence of the neo-
Guelph failure. Now, for the first time, there was an open
conflict between national governmental policies and the
Roman Curia. This liberal ecclesiastical policy went together
with a policy of economic renewal: free trade, stimulation
of productive energies, increasing the wealth of the country,
railroads, banks, public works, and modern changes in agriculture. Liberalism and free trade went together, as they had in
the Europeanism of the Risorgimento before 1848.

The parliamentary instrument of this policy was the
connubio, by which the much-vituperated Left, despite its
solemn and repeated excommunication as demagogic, got into
the government—if not the whole Left, at least Rattazzi's
politically conspicuous band. There was a broadening, a transformation of the ruling class. It was then that the aristocracy
really lost its monopoly in the Piedmontese state, and the
bourgeoisie took over the government. There was no true,
genuine democracy as yet; that would have been inconsistent
with restricted suffrage, and with the tendencies not only of
Cavour but even of Rattazzi, who, after his democratic stand
in 1848, became even more conservative. But if democracy was not achieved—that was to be the task of a united
Italy—beginnings were made; the basis was established. That
had to be the case in a development that was after all liberal,
given the indissoluble bond between democracy and liberalism
(a bond not of static identity, but dialectic and dynamic).
There was no genuine republican party in Piedmont to
stimulate the democratic process. There was one at Genoa,

but it had no great influence on the general political situation. Moreover, Cavour fought it rabidly, and not always in a dignified way. He seemed to become dogmatic and antiliberal when dealing with it, tending to make a "taboo" of monarchy; i.e., tending to deny republicans a place within the free play of political forces. This tendency lived on for a long time even after the formation of the Kingdom of Italy.

Despite these limitations, the experiment of free government in Piedmont between 1850 and 1859, carried out essentially under Cavour's direction, was serious and fruitful. It was an integral and fundamental part of the Risorgimento, because it enabled Piedmont to maintain and strengthen the initiative taken with the war of 1848–49. Even more important, it realized the capacity of the Italians for self-government and showed it to the world, confirming their right to independence, which is both the premise and the result of self-government. In fact, if the primary condition for self-government is that a people not be subject to a foreigner, it would be futile for that people to remove itself from subjection if it were going to be enslaved at home. The presence of exiles from other Italian regions, their participation in journalism, in parliament, and in all forms of public life, even government, efficiently promoted the de-Piedmontization of the subalpine kingdom (which Gioberti had called for), and made of it an embryonic representation of all Italy. It has been opportunely pointed out recently that in fact it was precisely the new national consciousness and the elevation of political life under the liberal regime that brought about a true fusion of the aggregate of Cisalpine states comprising the Savoyard Kingdom. It promoted the modernization of the state, whose legislation even Cavour recognized as inferior to that of Naples. In other words, if Piedmont took up the cause of Italy, and helped further the liberal-constitutional experiment by contributing to it the serious and sedate temperament of its people, as well as the compactness of its state and dynasty, it is also true that Italy of the Risorgimento, striding toward unity, promoted the perfection of the Piedmontese state, and its political, cultural, and moral elevation.

4. *The Important Function of the Action Party*

A consequence of this policy was the elevation of Piedmont on the Italian and on the international level. It was a small state, maintaining liberty and a constitution on the borders of the Austrian Empire, during a period of European political reaction. These things made it even more important to behave prudently in the matter of the national program. Piedmont was to be the champion of Italy tacitly, by example. The status quo of the treaties was the basis for relations between Italy and the powers, and Austria was encamped on the Ticino. For Piedmont to protest to Vienna against the illegal confiscation of goods belonging to Lombards who had emigrated to Piedmont and become Sardinian citizens—a protest pushed to the point of recalling the Sardinian ambassador—was to do a great deal. Even a liberal domestic policy had to be enunciated and carried out with prudence; but a liberal, or national, foreign policy could only be implied, or at most hinted at by the Piedmontese government.

That policy was expressed openly in Italy and abroad by the Action Party, and above all by Mazzini. It was done not just with domestic and foreign propaganda, but through attempts at insurrection as well. Taken one by one, Mazzini's attempts can easily be criticized, his *coups de main* considered mad. Nevertheless, it remains true that without the London Committee and its manifestoes, without Mazzini's loan bonds and the martyrs of Belfiore, without the Milanese sixth of February, without Pier Fortunato Calvi and the efforts in the Lunigiana, the Italian question would not have been kept before Europe. If it had not been for the hotheads (as the young Finali said to Cavour, who had to agree), Cavour would not have been able to propound the cause of Italy at the

Congress of Paris. Nor was it merely a question of the relationship between the implicit and the explicit, or between those responsible for the conduct of government and those who were free to act as they wanted. There was much more: the program of the Risorgimento in its entirety—that is to say, as a total change and integral reconstruction of Italy on an ethical-political level—is to be found in Mazzini and, with a great difference in spirit and structure but with no less breadth of inspiration, in the radical-liberals, who were closely following the lead of Piedmontese governmental reforms, whereas moderate thought became ever more opportunistic and diplomatic, and was losing importance compared to what it had been before 1848. Even in the subalpine parliament and in its journalism, the Left played a propulsive role, which has been ignored by most and neglected by scholars, blinded by Cavour's bright star. The Left moved within the ambit of constitutional monarchy, and was neither Mazzinian nor Ferrarian; but it drew its inspiration from Mazzinianism and from radical liberalism.

The major and most fruitful attempt to fuse the Action Party and Piedmontese politics, to fuse Mazzini (or at least the Mazzinians) and Cavour, was made by the National Society. The significance of the Society was contained in that quasi ultimatum delivered by the founder Manin to the House of Savoy: "Make Italy and I am with you. If not, not." Despite the energetic clarity of that dilemma, there was nevertheless some ambiguity possible: was there to be unity, or simply unification? Manin preferred to use the latter term, but other declarations and the whole tendency of the Society dissolved all reservations. The program of the Society came to consist in asking Piedmont to be absorbed by Italy, renouncing its existence and its particularistic traditions; at the same time, the Society asked all Italians to renounce federalism, republican or monarchical, in favor of the Savoyard monarchy. Aside from this last point, the other elements of the program were purely Mazzinian; and in fact there were some precedents in Mazzini even for that point, to be found in his attitude toward Charles Albert in 1848. It could well be said that Piedmont and Cavour were adhering to the Mazzinian program by accepting the program of the National Society. There is no continuity, there is only a great jump between the Savoyard political policy of all 1849 (in fact, up to and after the Congress of Paris) and the political line from 1859 on. The decisive push for that jump came from Mazzini, and more generally from the republican Action Party.

5. *From the Crimean War to the War in Lombardy*

We must check every link in what is accepted as the iron and golden chain of events in common Risorgimento historiography: Cavour's ministry—Crimean War—Congress of Paris —French-Sardinian alliance and war of 1859. It is not yet quite clear whether it was Cavour or Victor Emmanuel who first had the idea of letting Piedmont participate in the Crimean War; but the question is not important here. What is important is to determine the exact national and international framework of that participation. From the ideological point of view, the war of the two Western Powers against Russia presented two stages: in the first, there was an emphasis on liberal idealism as opposed to czarism, and hints at an appeal to the movement for the liberation of peoples: in other words, a resumption of 1848. If Austria had made common cause with Russia, even if only in the form of a benevolent neutrality, France and England would have had no choice but to arouse all the oppressed nations, from the Poles to the Serbs, against the renewed Holy Alliance. But Austria "astonished the world with its ingratitude": her neutrality was hostile to Russia, to the point of threatening intervention (a threat that aroused great hopes among the Western Powers). Under these circumstances, the participation of Piedmont was a guarantee offered by the Western Powers to Austria that she would have nothing to fear in Italy; in other words, it had a pro-Austrian aspect. Even if there had been no other motives, we can well understand the opposition not only of Mazzini but of the Piedmontese Left.

The results were the military resurgence of Piedmont after the defeat at Novara, the reconfirmed and strengthened relations with the Western Powers, the participation of Piedmont at the Congress of Paris, and the discussion of the Italian question there. But whoever would conclude that Italian independence and unity issued from the Crimean War would be committing something worse than an exaggeration. There is not a single thread that leads from the Congress of Paris to the war of 1859. In Paris, Cavour did indeed try to transform the temporary military alliance of the war into a general and permanent understanding for the solution of the Italian question, and he gained England most of all. (At the same time, in a difficult balancing act, he caressed Russia.) But after all the sanguine hopes of the first moment, the attempt proved to be a clear failure. The period from the close of the Congress of Paris to the battle of Magenta is by no means characterized by a Franco-English understanding against Austria and on the side of Piedmont; instead, England detached itself from France and drew closer to Austria, whereas France and Piedmont drew closer to Russia.

The war of 1859 broke out under the double sign of the Franco-Russian understanding and of opposition to the war on the part of the Derby-Disraeli ministry. It was only the return of Palmerston to power, in June, 1859, that brought about the change in English policy. Even the common attitude of France and England toward the Bourbons in those years made no real contribution to the Risorgimento, nor was it a conspicuous asset to Cavour's politics. Beneath the identity of their protest against the Bourbon system, there was the difference in the interests of the two powers, their rivalry in the Mediterranean. In Naples in those years, there was growing sentiment in favor of a party that would have liked to replace the Bourbons with a Murat. Their triumph would have meant the complete enfeoffment of Italy to France, with an allied-subordinate prince in the North, and one in the South who was bound even more tightly by family ties. It is to Mazzini's highest credit that he saw the mortal danger of Muratism for the Italian Risorgimento, and did what he could to avert it. Cavour was also not unaware of that danger; but because he did not feel strong enough to fight it directly, he tried to get England to settle it. With the expedition to Sapri (condemned by moderate liberals, at least the Genoese episode), Mazzini and Pisacane tried to trip the Muratists; and their action had its effects both on patriotic Italian public opinion and on the policy of Napoleon III, who was again prompted to provide for Italy.

The attempt by Orsini proved to be the final spur to Napoleon III. Whether it aroused him in the political-ideal sense, or whether it aroused personal preoccupations for his safety, the fact is that the attempt brought about the compact of Plombières, which is the true point of departure for 1859, and for the fulfillment of the Italian political Risorgimento. None of this was a direct continuation of the Crimean War or the Congress of Paris, but rather a new beginning. The beginning was made by Napoleon III, but was decisively influenced by the Action Party and Mazzini. The fact that he had nothing to do with Orsini's attempt does not change anything: for Napoleon III, the attempt—very rightly—fitted into the general framework of Mazzinian action.

6. *Mazzini and Cavour*

We must not conclude from all this that there was a real, if not personal, complementary relationship between Mazzini and Cavour in his later period, or we shall fall back into the territorial-Savoyard conception of the Risorgimento. In fact, it would be very easy for that conception to combine the work of Mazzini and Cavour, and to have these two men embrace each other in history, though they so cordially hated each other in life. (In practice, those who hold that conception prefer to eliminate Mazzini as much as possible.) No one would think of denying that Mazzini was the oldest and most tenacious propagandist of Italian unity and of the unified Italian state. No one could or does contest the highly important effectiveness of his work in that direction. And no one, furthermore, can doubt that a unified Italian state arose between 1859 and 1861 (Venice and Rome being the completions of an already existing edifice) around the nucleus of the Piedmontese state; and that this work of unificatory aggregation was carried out under the political and governmental direction of the Count of Cavour.

If the question is put this way, we need only discuss the how and the when, the more and the less, of the two men's actions: when did Cavour convert to the cause of Italian unity; what role did he play in the expedition of the Thousand; who is responsible for the idea and the initiative of the expedition to the Marches and to Umbria; how was the proclamation of Rome as the capital of Italy arrived at, and so on. These particulars are undoubtedly of great interest, but the differing answers to them do not radically change the general view. If the Risorgimento is considered to be fully realized in 1870 according to the only realization possible, all the programs and forces that went into it would appear to be purely and simply absorbed and "overcome."

However, if we go beyond a simple political-territorial consideration, it must be established that the unified-monarchical-constitutional-parliamentary Italian state formed in 1860–70 presents certain characteristics that are opposed to Mazzini's ideas and programs. Though we may discuss the role each one played in bringing about unity, it is simply not correct to say that Mazzini and Cavour each contributed to a result which, by unifying their work, entirely transcended and absorbed them. In reality, there was a battle between them; and Cavour was the winner, Mazzini the loser. To be more exact, Mazzini was the winner at first, when he imposed his unitary program on Piedmontese "municipalism"; but when it came to executing this program, Mazzini had to yield. And (let us say it quickly so that we do not have to return to it) radical liberalism, or republican-federal autonomism, had to yield even more.

In bringing about Italian unity, the point was how, by whom, and for whom this unity was to be brought about. The question of monarchy or republic contained an even more profound contrast between Cavour and Mazzini. The *idée fixe* of Mazzini was popular Italian initiative: and if, from an international point of view, it meant that Italy had to "do it alone" before the other peoples, from a domestic point of view it meant that it was up to the Italian people to rise and bring about unity. "Revolutions must be made by the people and for the people." That was why he reproached King Victor Emmanuel, in his open letter dated September 20, 1859, in Florence: "You did not unite with the people of Italy, nor did you call them to join you. Seduced by the sorry politics of a minister who preferred the arts of Ludovico il Moro to the role of regenerator, you refused the arm of our people, and needlessly, in an ill-starred moment, called in the arms of a foreign tyrant to help in the enterprise of liberation."

Once again, we must not reduce the dissension between Mazzini and Cavour to a simple difference of practical appraisal, with Mazzini believing that Italy could work alone against Austria (as Charles Albert had affirmed), whereas Cavour thought not. Nor can it be simply reduced to a contrast between the doctrinaire Mazzini, who refused any contribution from a "tyrant," and the opportunistic Cavour. Over and above all this, Mazzini intuited, with the clairvoyance of his passion, that the French alliance was something more than a practical expedient: it was the means by which the national-popular cause of Italy would be transformed into a monarchical-governmental enterprise. In discussing the treaty for the cession of Nice and Savoy, Cavour said in the Senate, on June 9, 1860: "Senator Pallavicino loves the alliance with the revolution first, and then the one with France." These were not meant as words of praise for Pallavicino, since Cavour's preference was just the opposite. He would have as little as possible to do with revolution, even with national revolution. In fact, several times he opposed the word "national" to "revolutionary," taking the former adjective to mean the monarchical-national movement in favor of the House of Savoy. It is known that Cavour considered it absolutely necessary to take the audacious step of having Piedmont renew the war against Austria alone if Garibaldi and the Action Party triumphed in the Kingdom of Naples, so as to give the lost initiative in the national movement back to the monarchy. "For a prince of Savoy, it is better to die in a war than in a revolution."

The struggle between Mazzini and Cavour, then, was a struggle between two initiatives: the popular-revolutionary initiative (which Mazzini meant to maintain even if the monarchy were accepted), and the monarchical-governmental initiative. In that consisted their irreconcilability. Mazzini's policy between Villafranca and the Neapolitan plebiscite was a policy of neutrality between republic and monarchy, trying to get the final decision assigned to the vote of a constituent national assembly. He had no doubt as to how the vote would go, but he maintained that a monarchy instituted *ex novo* by popular vote would be one thing, and the aggregation of the various parts of Italy around an already existing monarchy would be another. Cavour and Victor Emmanuel also recognized the difference; but the guidelines for conduct they drew from it were just the opposite. We must not think that Cavour was not completely solid in his monarchical and dynastic sentiments just because he had detested Charles Albert and been detested in return, or because he did not always get along perfectly well with Victor Emmanuel. The abiding antirepublicanism of Cavour (except for a brief period—or, rather, moment—in his early youth) went hand in glove with his anti-revolutionism, with his aversion to popular government and popular initiative, and was certainly tied to his fear of communism (see above, pp. 136–7).

Nevertheless, Cavour's anti-revolutionary sentiments, his decided aversion to popular initiative, and his dominant preoccupation with keeping the leadership of the national movement in the hands of the monarchical government did not follow solely from his dynastic and conservative interests. There was something of a liberal element in all of it. In September, 1860, at the time of the acute conflict with Garibaldi, he said that it was not merely a question of persons, but of two contrasting systems: Garibaldi was dreaming of some sort of dictatorship, without a parliament and with little liberty. (In fact, Garibaldi's tendency toward a "national dictatorship" was utilized by Victor Emmanuel and by Cavour in favor of the monarchy.) A little later, in his famous letter of September 29, 1860, to the Countess of Circourt, Cavour presents liberty and a dictatorship of popular origin as antitheses. Rejecting General Filangieri's advice to make himself dictator, he proclaims his faith in liberal parliamentarianism in eloquent words, with an almost lyrical tinge. But if Cavour had faith in parliament, Mazzini maintained his aversion for constitutional monarchy. He had expressed his first thoughts on the subject back in 1834: "Constitutional monarchy is the most immoral form of government in the world; it is an essentially corrupting institution, for the organized struggle that constitutes the vitality of that government excites all the individual passions toward the conquest of honors, or of wealth, which alone gives access to honors."

With this we come to a fundamental contrast of ideas—let us even say of "views of the world"—between the two men. Cavour never fled from the "organized struggle," even if he sometimes changed the rules of the game, as in the persecution of the "Italy of the People." And he was by no means scandalized by that "excitement" of the individual passions, as was the moralist Mazzini. He once said in parliament that it was impossible to imagine an order founded on liberty where there were not parties and struggles. Complete and absolute peace was not compatible with liberty, which had to be accepted with its benefits, "and perhaps also with its drawbacks." Mazzini also intended to maintain liberty, but his goal was an order in which the struggle (of parties) would naturally cease. "Duty, once accepted, excludes the possibility of struggle." That was Mazzini's ideal of unity, his "dogma" of unity, as he called it. As we know, for him it went far beyond political unity, which he considered but one element of moral and religious unity.

There is, then, a double aspect to the dissension between Mazzini and Cavour: on the one hand, Mazzini is the more liberal, the more radical innovator, inasmuch as he propounds popular initiative as compared with Cavour, the jealous custodian of governmental-monarchical initiative; on the other hand, the assessment must be reversed because of the ideal of uniformity envisioned by Mazzini as his goal, in contrast to the incessant political struggle envisioned by Cavour. This latter contrast derives from the very mental structure of the two men: Cavour rationalistically distinguishes between politics and religion (or ethics), whereas Mazzini unifies them mystically. Rationalistic secularism and religious mysticism are undoubtedly outstanding and opposed characteristics of Cavour and Mazzini, though Cavour was by no means indifferent to religious problems. (In fact, as we shall see, his ideas reached their greatest heights precisely in that area.) Nor does this antithesis of mental structure and spiritual aspirations in the two men necessarily signify an intrinsic and irreducible opposition of their different aspirations; for they represent equally profound and equally necessary needs in the course of history. From this point of view, we can indeed speak of

Mazzini and Cavour as complementary, but on a much higher level than that of immediate political accomplishments.

7. *Garibaldi*

In the contest between Mazzini and Cavour, between the national assembly as realizer of popular initiative and the plebiscitary system as the democratic means for consecrating the monarchical initiative, the man who tipped the scales in favor of the latter was Garibaldi. And that, even though he proclaimed himself a republican, and though he opposed Cavour almost as much as he did Mazzini. In his famous toast delivered in London in 1864, Garibaldi proclaimed that Mazzini was his teacher. But later, when the differences with Mazzini (and even more with the Mazzinians) had become poisoned and gangrenous, he chose to retract, saying he had been an Italian and a republican since infancy, and that he owed nothing to Mazzini. As a matter of fact, Mazzini truly had been the teacher of Garibaldi, as of so many others; but the spiritual make-up of his disciple was, and remained, profoundly different from his own.

Garibaldi was the ideal leader for a war of the people; he was a *condottiero* capable of dragging and guiding individual citizens onto the field of battle, capable of inflaming them for the national cause and yoking them to it, all with complete personal disinterest, and with ingenuous heroism. He embodied the national-popular Italian spirit, longing for independence, liberty, and justice, in all its primitive force, in all its immediate purity. He was much closer to the people than Mazzini; he understood them better and they him. But precisely because he incorporated so well the popular consciousness in all its ingenuousness, he was not able to rise above it, to direct it toward far-off, ultimate goals. He was a marvelous realization of the second part of Mazzini's diptych "thought and action," but not of the first. Though he had a much more realistic temperament than Mazzini, he was much less profound and farsighted. Mazzini's concept of the self-creation of the people eluded him, and the ultimate religious foundation of Mazzini's program remained foreign to him. Though he sincerely believed in the superiority of a republic, he made the very sensible affirmation that it was impossible to proclaim a republic in 1860. At the same time, he broadened the concept of republic to include any government approved by the people. (If the English, he used to say, are content with the government of Queen Victoria, it must be considered a republic.) Because of this, he believed firmly that the plebiscites were the consecration of Victor Emmanuel's monarchy, without giving much thought to the particular conditions under which the plebiscites were held (cf. below, p. 166), or to the ultimate political need represented by Mazzini's demand for a constituent assembly, which he thought was a waste of time. Once he had recognized that he could not proceed from Naples to Rome and Venice, he saw no reason to hold up the annexations. For him, the political dimensions of the problem disappeared behind the territorial. This way of looking at things was due in part to his conviction that a temporary dictatorship was necessary if the Italian nation (or any other) was to be founded. In this case, it was to be the dictatorship of Victor Emmanuel. He did not stop to consider that it was not a matter of temporary dictatorship, but a permanent dynastic foundation. Only later, after 1870, did Garibaldi, like Mazzini, speak of the insufficiency of the Sardinian constitution, and of the need to replace it with a national compact.

8. *European Politics after 1848: From the Peoples to the Governments*

The disagreement between Mazzini and Cavour on what line to take to solve the Italian question is tied to, or forms part of, their different method, their different vision of European politics. This difference, like the previous one, also derives from the difference in moral temperament between the two men, but is at the same time connected with the entire development of Europe before and after 1848. I must repeat here what I wrote in an article in February, 1935, and have since repeated several times.

It is superficial and only partly correct to conceive of the period between 1859 and 1870, the period that realized Italian and German unity, as no more than the continuation and fulfillment of the national programs formulated in the preceding period, up to and including 1848. As a matter of fact, there is a profound difference between the earlier programs and the later realizations. In the earlier period, the promoters of the various national movements had dreamed of a free Europe, solidly reorganized through the works of fraternal peoples. Mazzini gave the classic, the most splendid formulation of that program, and raised it to a metaphysical, religious plane, with his conception of the peoples as the various members of a single body, the body of humanity. As he was well aware, this conception was similar to the New Testament idea that Christians constitute the body of Christ. But even without ascending to those dizzy heights, the national and social agitators contemporary to Mazzini felt and expressed as intensely as he did this solidarity among the European peoples, this unity of the individual national causes. In fact, we have seen that even outside the ranks of the agitators, amidst the moderate Italian writers, we find (though no longer on a democratic-revolutionary level) the fundamental idea of spiritual European unity, the close tie between the affairs of Italy and of Europe, and the Italian task of rejoining Europe and serving the development of European civilization.

After 1850, the character of the national movements tends to change from popular and solidary to governmental, with each of the movements tending to move within its own limited sphere. Popular initiative is replaced by the initiative of heads of state or governments, men who continue to look for international connections and keep watch on them, but only as political opportunities to be exploited for individual national-statist aims. Characteristic, for example, is the difference in 1859 between Kossuth, who sought to get France and Piedmont to make Hungarian independence an objective of the war, and Napoleon III, who considered Hungarian independence no more than a pawn to be played in winning the war in Lombardy. In 1859, too, Napoleon III and Cavour cared about nothing but reassuring the czar that Polish volunteers would not be allowed to fight in Lombardy. Each national cause now proceeded on its own, and the abandonment of one was used to serve the advantage of the other.

Mazzini remained ever faithful to the European-democratic conception of nationality. He continued to look at all of Europe at the same time; and not for the sole purpose of espying opportunities for exploiting the various European situations in favor of Italy, but out of a profound consciousness of the solidarity of the fates of the various nations. For him, it was always a matter of the international of peoples against the international of kings. In fact, this tendency in Mazzini seems to get stronger with the passage of time. There is a letter he wrote after 1860, in which he says, more or less, that his head aches because it is filled with the great confusion of peoples, popular movements, and insurrections taking place or being prepared in half of Europe. Up to his death, Mazzini continued to see the Italian Risorgimento tied to the dissolution of the Hapsburg Empire; and that in turn was tied to the dissolution of the Turkish Empire. He saw the liberation and the national reconstruction of the people of Poland and Greece within one framework. He was particularly insistent in maintaining that it was the special mission of Italy to favor the liberation and the national fulfillment of the Slavic peoples, and to draw close to them. On this score, too, the conception and method of Napoleon III and Cavour triumphed over Mazzini; and, as always happens to those who triumph, they got the unanimous applause that goes with the *fait accompli*. And yet an important consequence of this triumph was that although some national problems were resolved, others were only put off. Italy and Germany were unified; the grand European plan for the dissolution of the Hapsburg and Turkish empires, and for their reconstruction as federations of peoples, was put aside. But the deferred problems remained: later, they became acute, no longer postponable, and we got the European war of 1914.

9. *Napoleon III and Mazzini*

For Mazzini, then, there was a triple reason for combating the royal-Cavourian policy of alliance with Napoleon III: it meant (1) a foreign rather than national initiative; (2) alliance with despotism and exclusion of popular initiative; (3) mutilation of the European program of the nationalities.

One of the points of view from which to look at European history in the second half of the nineteenth century is that of the antithesis and at the same time affinity between Mazzini and Napoleon III. Louis Napoleon was a man who was morally—and perhaps historically—vastly superior to "the Great" Napoleon. Whereas the first Napoleon never thought of anything but his career and greatness (or, at best, about the material greatness of France), Louis Napoleon had sincere European and human interests, and genuinely felt certain ideals. Evidence of his sincerity is the lack of poses and of *mise en scène*, so dear to his uncle. Louis Napoleon glimpsed more than one of the chief aspects of the European problem: liberation of the nationalities as the basis for a new and peaceful settlement of Europe, elevation of the working masses, the fruitful soundness of international free trade. (The commercial treaty of 1860 between England and France remains one of the best things accomplished in Europe during this period.) The first and the second point were objectives he had in common with Mazzini. In short, as we have already indicated, the program which French democracy had refused to accept in 1848 was taken on by Napoleon III, at least to a certain extent. But there was a basic difference in spirit between Napoleon III and Mazzini: the one was authoritarian and Caesarean, whereas the other was democratic and religious. Each considered the other a great enemy: the poor, seemingly isolated, defenseless exile in London was one of the greatest and most constant worries of Napoleon III. They were fighting over who was to have the European initiative, Caesarism or "God and the people," and whether Europe was to arise only for the people or also through the people.

Their biggest quarrel was over Italy. If one looks at it carefully and dispassionately, there were, properly speaking, two initiatives taken in the decisive phase of the Italian question, and they were taken by Napoleon III and Mazzini. The Savoyard monarchy and even Cavour himself just went along; their action was the effect and, so to speak, the resultant of the two vectors. However, Cavour and the monarchy moved from third place to first, thanks to Cavour's capacity for arranging and achieving things and thanks to his supreme equilibrium and his liberal inspiration. Napoleon III understood that his own fortunes were tied to the solution of the Italian problem; in fact, he fell because he stopped before taking the final step, thus remaining a victim of absolutistic clericalism and the temporal power. Mazzini shook with rage at the idea that a despot, a foreigner to boot, should be the one to mold the new Italy by hitching it to his own wagon, taking its soul so that it might have its body. In his eyes, Cavour and the Savoyard monarchy were the necessary accomplices in this enslavement and treachery. Ever watchful of Mazzini, and stimulated not only by the desire to forestall him but also (we believe, despite any other opinion on this matter) by the fear of being assassinated by the Action Party, Napoleon III tore the initiative from the hands of the London conspirator. (We have already noted that the negotiations at Plombières took place

only a few months after the assassination attempt by Orsini.)
But though he took the initiative away from Mazzini, he could
not develop it integrally because of the intrinsic flaw of his
regime, which would have liked to bring about European
democratic liberalism using nationalistic and authoritarian
means.

10. Analysis of the Plebiscitary Unification

In the amazingly short period between April, 1859, and March,
1861—in fact, we should say October, 1860—Italian unity was
realized. It had not existed since the Lombard invasion thirteen
centuries before, and had never existed as unitary political
autonomy. That consideration alone suffices to show the absurdity of the thesis (if it deserves the honor of that name)
which would like to reduce the Risorgimento to the course of
territorial expansion of the Savoyard state. After having taken
seven hundred years to go from the Alps to the Ticino, that
state, by its miraculous intrinsic force, is supposed to have
swallowed the rest of Italy in two years. This enormous dis-
proportion cannot be explained unless we understand that
completely different and deeper forces played a part in the
unification. It was a completely ethical-political, centuries-old
process which, because of a concurrence of circumstances, was
able in two years to achieve a territorial-political result that
was an essential but by no means unique or supreme part of
the Risorgimento. The prodigious rapidity of this realization
ought in fact to be another reason to investigate whether there
was not some constitutional defect hidden in it.

Those extraordinary concurrent circumstances included:
popular initiative (the revolutions in Central Italy, the expedition of the Thousand, plans and attempts to completely
overthrow the temporal power); the political and military action of the Savoyard monarchy; manifold elements in the European situation—i.e., aside from the French-Piedmontese al-

liance and the entire policy of Napoleon III, the policy of Palmerston and Russell favoring Italian unity; the internal Austrian crisis; dissension between Austria and Prussia and, even more, the dissension between Austria and Russia. In that fatidical two-year period, the monarchy, with Cavour acting for it, acts as mediator (in its own interests as well as those of Italy) between the popular initiative and European politics. The mediation was a work of extraordinary political ability, superior to the most beautiful diplomatic achievements of Bismarck because of the complexity of the elements it had to reconcile. But there could have been no mediation without the terms to be mediated. Now, the popular initiative came from Mazzini—or was at least directly or indirectly of Mazzinian inspiration and provenience (recall what we said about the National Society). If there was another influence aside from the Mazzinian, it was the influence of radical liberalism. It is therefore distinctly antihistorical to bestow honor on the demiurge or *deus ex machina* Victor Emmanuel or Cavour by considering the action of Mazzini after 1849 (and particularly in the decisive two-year period) as ineffective or downright harmful, an obstacle to the work achieved.

The most important event leading to Italian unity was not the Franco-Piedmontese war against Austria in 1859, which by itself would only have produced (and in the formal intentions of Napoleon III was only meant to produce) a kingdom of Northern Italy and a confederation—or, in other words, a return to the first phase of 1848. Three events were basic for Italian unity: the insurrections in Central Italy, the expedition to Sicily, and the expedition to the Marches and Umbria. They were three thought-actions inspired by Mazzini, and each of them was popular-revolutionary. Moreover, the first two, at least initially, were carried out as popular revolution. (Keep in mind that the Tuscan revolution of April 27, the most important of the Central Italian revolutions, was the work of the Action Party.) In fact, the expedition of the Thousand is

the archetype of insurrection and popular war, with the popular hero par excellence, Garibaldi. The third event was the
work of the monarchy, which took over the idea and the actual
beginnings of the popular revolution. And the monarchy took
it over—read Cavour's letters of this time—because it believed
that this was the only way to save itself, because it did not want
Italian unity to be achieved by republicans. Once again, and
precisely at the right moment, the dilemma Victor Emmanuel
II had seen so clearly came up again: either king of Italy or
"milord Savoy."

Mazzini yielded and accepted the dominant participation of
the monarchy, and in fact promoted it, even though he foresaw a result contrary to his republican ideals, because his desire
for unity prevailed over everything else. In this case, it was to
be territorial unity rather than political-moral unity. To be
sure, he reserved the right of political opposition for himself
and his followers, which meant the right to continue making
propaganda for republican ideals. Mazzini, whom so many consider the intransigent sectarian, the pure adversary, the idealist
with his head in the clouds, saw the political reality and knew
how to adapt himself to it in the supreme interest of the nation. As a matter of fact, from his point of view, the question
to be asked is whether he did not adapt himself to it too
much. It was a magnanimous sacrifice, a grandiose case of
sic vos non vobis. Whence derives, then, the persistent dissension between him and the new order, a dissension that
made of the greatest apostle of the unitary state, once it was
realized, a conspirator and a reprobate unto death?

Mazzini had wanted the Italian people as a national community to determine their own political regime freely, directly,
and integrally; he called for a "national compact" dictated by
a constituent assembly. Even Gioberti had said in the
Rinnovamento that after the Piedmontese dictatorship, which
was necessary for the liberation and formation of Italy, the

political and legal disposition of the nation was to be the work of a universal diet of the nation. In Mazzini's eyes, the plebiscites were not the equivalent of a constituent assembly or of a compact, for several reasons: they were not preceded by discussions in the arena of free political struggle; their formulation did not pose any concrete alternative to union with the constitutional reign of Victor Emmanuel II; and, finally, they implied the pure and simple acceptance by all of Italy of a purely Piedmontese state, granted by royal concession. In his eyes, all this meant an exterior aggregation, almost a conquest, instead of the popular creation of a new Italy. Such an idea could only be confirmed when parliament (and it was a parliament elected by very limited suffrage), voting to establish the Kingdom of Italy, proclaimed the king Victor Emmanuel II, not I. Mazzini, republican federalists, and democrats in general considered it a continuation of the Savoyard monarchy, not the creation of a new Italian monarchy: divine right, not popular right. It was a divine right which, though coupled with the "will of the nation" (and understood to exclude papal theocracy), made an open and conspicuous show of itself in the formulation of the heading of all the legal documents of the new kingdom.

This judgment on the part of Mazzini cannot be considered (as "moderate liberals" liked to do and still do) simple a priori dogmatism or even sectarian distortion. It is necessary to distinguish in it two different judgments: one on the course of unification in 1860–61, considered *hic et nunc* in its immediate political-juridical reality; and the other on the future result of a unification that came about the way this one did—in other words, the potentialities that were or were not contained in the Italian state thus constituted, together with the possibilities for political action within the state itself. On the first point, the judgment of history coincides substantially with Mazzini's judgment (and with that of the republican federalists). It is an established fact (though open to interpretation either from the point of view of the Risorgimento or the anti-Risorgimento) that the annexationist, plebiscitary-parliamentary course by which the Kingdom of Italy was made was not a course taken by the Italian people with full enlightenment of conscience and freedom of will. Instead, it was a necessary improvisation, a compromise between popular forces and conservative, dynastic powers, made under the triple pressure of the only Italian state left on its feet, European diplomacy, and the lack of any immediately visible and acceptable solution other than a return to the earlier state of affairs, foreign occupation, or anarchy. Victor Emmanuel, Cavour, Garibaldi, Mazzini—everyone adopted the principle that "a thing done cannot be undone," which Gioberti had stressed in his *Rinnovamento*. The necessary improvisation translated itself into the imperfect character of the plebiscites, into their ratification by a parliament elected by limited suffrage, and into the pure and simple adoption of the constitution *granted* to Piedmont by Charles Albert in 1848—in other words, into all those features Mazzini disliked. Therefore, this improvisation was necessarily, *hic et nunc*, in the immediate political-juridical reality, not a true and genuine creation of the new national state, but precisely the annexation of the other Italian states to an already existing Italian state.

Because of his dogmatic and static mentality, Mazzini deduced from these established facts a definitive judgment of condemnation and an attitude of absolute intransigence toward the new state. His position toward the Kingdom of Italy was a return to the position of revolutionary intransigence he had held toward the old Italian states. Lacking, as he did, a certain kind of liberal mentality, he failed to see that through all the patching up of the old, there was a substantial innovation in the improvised construction, one that contained the potentiality of healing the defect of its origin. The innovation was the liberal regime, which, better than Achilles' lance, healed not only his own wounds but those of others as well. In the daily political struggle, it allowed the testing, modifying, and even the radical transformation of the construction itself. The daily political struggle would bring about the ratification or the rejection of that which had been put into the construction improvised by necessity. True, Mazzini was not the only one who took a dogmatic and static stance toward the Kingdom of Italy; it was also taken on the other side of the fence, perhaps even more firmly, by his moderate-liberal adversaries and even by the *ralliés* of the Action Party. For these last, in fact, the plebiscites were not an unfolding political act but an immobile fetish, for they considered the construction of 1860–61 a *noli me tangere*, and they saw the parliamentary oath as a juridical consecration of this untouchableness. Thus did they mutilate and falsify the concept of national sovereignty and initiative, which was the basis of the Risorgimento.

A most important consequence of the "construction of necessity"—i.e., of the formation of the Kingdom of Italy through the annexationist-parliamentary procedure we have described—was that the popular classes, not having participated directly in the construction, could not make their own interests felt in it. And so the new construction included nothing of the social program of the Risorgimento formulated by Mazzini, Ferrari, Gioberti in the *Rinnovamento*, and most ardently of all by Pisacane (a program that the moderates and even Cavour substantially ignored). This was the negative social aspect of "moderatism" and of the compromise character inherent in the Kingdom of Italy, an aspect complementary to the political aspect—or, rather (as we have already pointed out), a necessary consequence of it, since the principle of *politique d'abord* always holds true. But the remedial possibilities inherent in the liberal regime could be applied to this particular defect, just as they could to the general defects.

11. *Right and Left*

After 1861, a basic difference between Mazzini and the monarchical government concerned the method by which to complete national unity. This difference was but a particular instance of the general, pre-existing disagreements. If Mazzini had always maintained the principle *l'Italia farà da sè*, he had more reason to do so now that the Italian state included nearly the entire peninsula, with more than twenty million inhabitants. At most, he would concede a certain prudence with regard to Rome, for he did not ignore the possibility of an armed conflict with France and a war on two fronts, which might have meant the ruin of the unified state just when it had been achieved. As for Austria and Venetia, he had no doubts: there must be a direct duel between the old state and the new, with a popular insurrection leading the way, and with Italy joining the liberation movement of the peoples subject to the Hapsburgs. In this last period, Mazzini was more than ever faithful (as we already saw) to the idea of the solidarity of the peoples, despite the general evolution of European politics toward an opposite position. He always looked at Italy within the framework of a general European reconstruction based on nationalities, and he was always against nationalistic isolation.

These ideas were shared by the entire Action Party, which distinguished itself from the government moderates by its willingness to use the popular initiative without waiting for a nod from the government. But the Action Party did not have Mazzini's resolute and compact will; above all, it was not resolute and compact in the question of republicanism, which Mazzini brought up again after the September Convention, and especially after the setbacks of 1866. Next to Mazzini, the most important person in the Action Party was Garibaldi; as a matter of fact, for all practical purposes he was even more influential than Mazzini. But he preferred "Italy and Victor

Emmanuel" to "God and the People." Even after Aspromonte and Mentana, he was still willing to wait for the initiative of the king, whom he had always liked and trusted (though he was just as hostile toward the moderate government as Mazzini was). As for the republic, Garibaldi referred it to the future will of the Italian people.

12. The Roman Question

With regard to the Roman Question, the government and the Action Party disagreed not only on the method for taking Rome from the pope, but even on what attitude to take toward the pope and what to do with him once Rome had become Italian. This was not just a question of politics, but of religion; the religious problem of the Risorgimento and of all Italian history had reappeared. Neo-Guelphism was practically finished, except for some conciliatory aspirations still in existence among groups of Catholic nationalists, who had some influence, if not in the solution of the Roman Question, then in arranging a *modus vivendi* after it had been settled. The government's solution had been formulated by Cavour shortly before his death and bequeathed to the Right, who accepted it only with reservations.

It was the most exalted part of Cavour's political conception: boldy detaching himself from moderate empiricism, he rose to the heights of an ideal. His idea was that the application of liberal principles to relations with the religious society (in other words, a free Church in a free state) would have the effect of converting Catholicism and the papacy to the principles of liberty, and reconciling them with modern society. He was firm in his belief that papal antiliberalism was an effect of the temporal power; concordats and jurisdictional principles were necessary only so long as the pope held both powers in his hands. But once the cause disappeared, the effect would disappear, too. Cavour did not have a clear idea of

Roman Catholic principles concerning the Church as a perfect society, endowed with complete and autonomous legislative, judicial, coercive powers; nor did he really know the inner nature of canon law, according to which jurisprudence, in all its implications and manifestations, is an integral part of Catholicism. And so he thought that eliminating the temporal power and at the same time allowing freedom to the Church would bring about an accord between the two basic moral principles of society, religion and freedom. Nor did he consider this a distant, vague ideal, but a concrete and already existing possibility. Cavour was realistic, empirical, and diplomatic on the purely political level of the national question; but on the level of ecclesiastical politics he rose to a conception different in the concrete from Mazzini's conception, but kindred in spirit, for it, too, was concerned with a grand and supreme mission reserved to Italy for European and human civilization. The difference between the phrase "God and the People" and the phrase "Religion and Liberty" consisted in this: in the Mazzinian phrase, there was the ideal of a humanity totally and mystically associated, and a religion of humanity that absorbed politics; whereas in Cavour's phrase, we glimpse a future society in which the power of the state will have been returned to its function as a simple instrument for the peace, order, and security of human beings living together, a society in which individuals will collaborate freely and without obstacles toward a full development of spiritual values.

After the death of the master, the Cavourian Right abandoned his idealism (though Riscasoli made some vain attempts to maintain it). Instead, they brought the settlement of the Roman Question back to the level of political-ecclesiastical compromise. So far as the anticlerical, antipapal Action Party was concerned, it would not hear of any guarantees to the pope, or even of a free Church in a free state. It spoke of the total annihilation of the political papacy, their intransigent enemy, and envisaged the destruction of the spiritual papacy, not exactly by a direct act of force, but as a result of the abolition of the temporal power and by the reduction of the papacy to a regime under the common law. In the final analysis, Cavour's system also aimed at putting the Church under the common law; but the aim had a profoundly different spirit, inasmuch as he hoped the common-law regime would bring about a reflowering of Catholicism, not its disappearance. Everyone knows of Garibaldi's outbursts of rage against the papacy and the clergy, but they are not to be taken literally. More generally, the Action Party did not work effectively to realize its anticlerical program; and when it came to power as the Left, it followed the ecclesiastical policy of the Right.

Compared with Cavour, the only one who had an organic conception of ecclesiastical policy was Mazzini. He considered the separation of Church and state absurd, except as a temporary expedient. Church and state were like the soul and the body. Aging papal Catholicism was to be replaced by the new religion of "God and the People," the new revelation that was to come from the conscience of the people by divine guidance, and that was to give supreme significance to the Italian Risorgimento. Mazzini, therefore, bitterly opposed the doctrine of "a free Church in a free state," which he considered empty and atheistic. He considered it that because as usual he transported it, without even noticing—or, rather, in conformity with his usual principle of mystical unity—from the sphere of juridical and political relationships to the sphere of ultimate moral relationships. He was unable to see that the separation of Church and state envisaged by Cavour by no means precluded what he so rightly wanted; namely, the influence of religion on politics, the spiritual on the temporal, ideals on reality. In fact, the separation might even favor that influence, might render it more free and pure. In other words, it was an attempt to realize what Mazzini himself, in his theoretical effort to reconcile authority and liberty, was asking for when he wrote: "We wish to have one common thought bind us in activity toward a common object; but such a union must have our free consent, and that object must belong to everyone, not to a class or sect."

13. *From 1861 to 1870*

On the whole, the general political tone is lower in Italy after 1861. The people play an ever-decreasing role in public life, particularly in the completion of the national edifice. On the one hand, we have secret cabinet politics, which in the end means nothing but waiting for the repercussions of international changes. On the other hand, we have restricted, isolated uprisings and rash actions, like those that led to Aspromonte and Mentana. The internal elaboration of the new state was carried out almost exclusively by the government, with scarcely any participation by public opinion or even by parliament (which continued to be elected by very limited suffrage). This phenomenon, which might be called oligarchical involution, is not peculiar to the Italian Risorgimento; in fact, it is even more marked elsewhere, particularly in Germany. And it is linked to the transformation in the European political mood after 1848, which we discussed earlier.

Monarchical-governmental solutions triumphed everywhere and in everything. There was no insurrection in Rome or Venice, nor was there a general upheaval in the Austrian Empire. The liberation of Venetia was a purely diplomatic-military affair handled by governments, devoid of the slightest ethical-political dignity. It came after military defeats (neither shameful nor ruinous in themselves, though they became both because of the ineptitude of the high command), the national humiliation stemming from having to receive Venetia from the hands of the foreigner, and the renunciation of the Trentino and Venezia Giulia. Two attempts on Rome failed, without arousing any reaction in the Italian people; subjection to Napoleon III continued and was embodied in the September Convention, the object of the imprecations of Mazzini and the entire Action Party; negotiations with Austria and France for a diplomatic solution of the Roman Question failed. It was only the war of 1870 that brought Rome to Italy; and even then, the government first had to reconfirm the September Convention. Even at the last moment, there was no popular insurrection in Rome; everyone waited for the royal troops. Then came the last plebiscite, and the transfer of the capital; and no one paid any attention to Mazzini's call for a constituent assembly. In the settlement with the pope, the Law of Guarantees adopted Cavour's solution, but reduced it to simple terms of *modus vivendi*, renouncing any idea of reforming Catholicism.

14. *The Post-Risorgimento*

After 1870, that lowering of tone we saw after 1861 becomes general. There are two contrasting interpretations of the phenomenon: the first sees it as having adverse consequences for the whole period of Italian political life from 1870 to the war, and tries to establish an opposition between the Risorgimento, which it does not want to repudiate, and the liberal-democratic regime that resulted from it; the other interpretation says that by this time the larger questions and the basic problems were resolved, and those that remained or those that would come up were not so grave or urgent. Everyday life was succeeding the heroic life of the Risorgimento. Substantially, the second interpretation is the true one: but we must distinguish and define.

The political-moral construction could not end with the political-territorial construction. Even if we do not accept Azeglio's simplicistic formula ("Italy is made; now the Italians must be made"), the very fact that the second construction was completed so hurriedly might make one suspect that there was still a great deal to do for the first. Mazzini expressed sad disappointment over the Italy that had been achieved, which was so far removed from the Italy of his dreams. He gave concrete political expression to the somewhat vague disappointment (which in itself might simply derive from the difference between any ideal and reality) by continuing to hope that, beyond the unified state, there would come a national society that realized the next degree in the divine plan, while in the bosom of that society the free exchange of ideas would be preparing for even higher degrees. In Mazzini's thought, this conception was a substitute, though on a higher level, for the liberal-constitutional conception of two parties alternating in power.

Even those who do not accept the details of Mazzini's ethical-political ideology must face the problem of the continuity of the Risorgimento and the post-Risorgimento. More precisely, one must ask whether the bases for subsequent development were effectively and sufficiently established with unification, and whether the development itself proceeded from those bases. The problem can be given concrete form under three headings: cultural, ethical-religious, and political in the precise sense. We must limit ourselves here to very rapid strokes, examining the problem especially in the fifty-year period that extends from the unification to the First World War.

There is no doubt that Italian cultural life in this period partook effectively and fruitfully of the cultural life of Europe, on a footing of spiritual and structural equality. One may discuss the how and the how much, but not the fact itself. It is not a simple chronological relationship, but an intimate bond that joins the Risorgimento and the Europeanization of Italian culture. This was precisely the European program which we have already seen was common to all currents of thought and action in the Risorgimento. Sometimes it was formulated as the return of Europe to Italy, as it was in the overweening patriotism of Mazzini and in the grandiosely baroque construction of Gioberti's *Primato*; and sometimes it was expressed as the need to bring Italy back to Europe, as was the case with the moderates, the radicals, the Gioberti of the *Rinnovamento*, and in Mazzini's more dispassionate thought and practical behavior. Certainly we can say that in the field of culture the Risorgimento laid the necessary and sufficient basis for the development of a unified Italy, and that the basis supported a blossoming of literature, art, and science on a European level, coming ever closer to the level of the most advanced countries. If we compare the ultimate inspiration of the first and second halves of the nineteenth century, the spiritual tone seems in some ways to decline. But we must keep in mind that, in the first place, that was true in all of Europe, not just in Italy; and in the second place, that any process of diffusion of culture almost inevitably leads to a certain lowering of quality, though that does not mean the process is any less physiological, any less progressive.

The ethical-religious aspect is the one that makes the lamentations of decline after 1870 easier and more frequent, and the one that was the object of most of Mazzini's recriminations. But it was also the one to which the rule mentioned earlier applies most; namely, that a certain decline was in the very nature of things, and must therefore be considered a physiological process of growth, not of decay. The period of intense, continuous, and mortal struggle was studded with conspiracies, insurrections, wars, with written and oral propaganda that was also a form of battle, and with necessary conflicts between the various national programs. Naturally such a period had a more intense rhythm of life, a faster pulse beat, higher flights of ideas, and more magnanimous impulses to action than the succeeding period of daily national life within the already realized construction, with its inevitable and quantitatively large portion of "routine."

If we really want to get at a fruitful spiritual evaluation of the post-Risorgimento, without getting lost in moralism and laments *temporis acti*, the question to be asked is this: does

Italian moral unity, the ultimate goal of the Risorgimento, maintain itself and progress in the succeeding period? We give a resolutely affirmative answer. From 1870 to 1914, the Italian national consciousness not only stood firm in the test of the daily task, which was so often monotonous and gray, but even enlarged and consolidated itself. Those who remember Italian life at the beginning of the century cannot help but support this judgment. Naturally there were depressing episodes and moments before and after 1900, but these do not contradict what we say, for we must look at the general tendency. Nor is the judgment contradicted by party struggles, even when they were very acute, for they are a condition and a consequence of a true national life. As Balbo said nearly a century ago, it would be impossible for everyone from one end of Italy to the other to see the welfare of the fatherland in the same way; and parties are nothing but different opinions on what constitutes the national welfare. The free expression of those opinions is one of the primary and most useful results of national liberty.

The conflict between Church and state, which culminated in the Roman Question, was the most delicate point for the Italian national conscience and for the moral unity of the nation in the post-Risorgimento period. In the first years after 1870, and especially in the capital city of Rome, it might well seem that an unbridgeable gap, an abyss had opened between "white" and "black" society, between two Italies. And yet that was not the case. Even then, even in the world that was between the Vatican and the Quirinal, and even for Pius IX and the Curia, the abyss was less deep than we might think. There was still an ultimate desire for a *modus vivendi*, which had been outlined in earlier days. There was the sense that the necessary legal-diplomatic arrangements were one thing, and that general daily life and innermost sentiments were another. With time, the scar healed ever more rapidly, the fusion became ever broader and more intimate. There was a system of "parallels"; that is to say, a genuine separation between Church and state, with no need to proclaim it. The system respectfully took account of essential ecclesiastical needs and of the religious life of the Italian people, and at the same time of the nonconfessionalism of the government. There was freedom of thought and conscience, free and peaceful discussion of all ideas; culture and modern consciousness moved forward. In that atmosphere, the Italian patriots divested themselves of their bristling and sectarian anticlericalism, which had been a weapon in the time of struggle; and the Italian Catholics, even the "clericals," gave up their prejudices and their partiality. They recognized that the Church had profited from the loss of temporal power, that the Law of Guarantees had not been and was not a diplomatic expedient or a legal illusion, but a genuine assurance of full freedom to the papacy. They moved ever closer to Italian life, to the point of participating in positions at the highest level immediately after the war.

Another major obstacle to Italian moral unity came from the "social question," the class conflict. Here, too, there was violent, intransigent opposition at first: the patriots attacked Socialism as though it were anarchy or high treason, and the Socialists spoke of the proletariat that has no fatherland. But here, too, intransigent opposition derived from mutual immaturity, occasional political battles, and the rhetoric of the party, and not from necessity or deep sentiments. In any case, those sentiments were modified on both sides, and with them the method of the conflict as well as the results. The very possibility of enunciating their claims and differences so clearly and crudely, and of taking action for the recognition of their demands, clarified the positions and brought men closer. The liberal regime showed itself ever more impartial in the social conflict, ever more hospitable toward the new classes and the new political forces. These, on the other hand, became ever more conscious of their ties to the common fatherland, and began to play an ever-growing role within the national framework.

By speaking of the entry of the proletariat into national life, we have passed on to the third point, which concerns the evolution of politics as such in the post-Risorgimento. Here the basic point was to get the people genuinely involved in the new state. It may be said that this was very imperfectly carried out, especially in the first decade. Given Italy's historical traditions, its small-town structure, and its geographical configuration, a very important question is that of local autonomy, or decentralization, as it is commonly and unhappily called. It was put aside almost without being examined, and that proved to be a grave lacuna in the course of the Risorgimento. Simple extension of the suffrage was delayed until 1882, even though France and Germany had had universal suffrage for some time, and electoral reforms had taken place in England. The indifference of the electoral body, as frequently evidenced by the large numbers of abstentions, showed that the higher level of consciousness among the upper classes had its limits, and emphasized the need for the broadening of suffrage. All this was a return to the Italian and European failure of 1848, to that rupture in the national development, to that change in the direction of European politics, to that incompleteness and imperfection in the plebiscitary and unificatory process, all of which we have discussed.

Still, we must not exaggerate. Civil liberties and parliament, the fundamental instruments for the elevation of the lower classes and their participation in political life, were assured and functioned well. Between 1870 and 1914, the constitutional monarchy on the whole showed a vitality of sorts, despite setbacks and grave crises (the second ministry of Crispi, 1898, the second ministry of Pelloux). These lasted only a short time, and did not damage the structure of the liberal regime; that is to say, they did not jeopardize the apparatus necessary for correcting mistakes and resuming the march forward. Though it was slow, the participation of the new strata in political life grew ever larger. After 1900 (as we mentioned earlier), when the proletariat enters the scene, participation becomes rapid and intense. And that was accompanied by the economic improvement and the general elevation of the living conditions of the lower classes. The tone of public life began to rise again, and the political struggle was resumed with fruitful intensity. Even before the war, there was nearly universal suffrage. Because the constitutional monarchy (after the uncertainties and temporary deviations alluded to above) adapted itself to—and, in fact, presided over—the liberal-democratic-social development, in keeping with the letter and the spirit of the constitution and the plebiscite, Mazzini's demand for a constituent assembly and a national compact was being resolved and absorbed, causing the republican party almost to disappear. In all three spheres, cultural, religious, and political, Italy on the eve of the First World War clearly possessed, in the achievements of the Risorgimento, the elements necessary to continue its process of political-spiritual development.

15. *The Traditions of the Risorgimento and the International Politics of the Italian State*

On the international level, the recently completed political-territorial Risorgimento bequeathed to the new state a material base, a political tactic, and several general guidelines. The material base was a unified Italy with twenty-six million inhabitants, who soon became thirty million and more. It was an Italy endowed with gradually increasing economic and technical strength, and growing military force. The base was not enough to make it pre-eminent among the already existing great powers, or even to compete with them; still, though it was the smallest among them, Italy was nonetheless a great power, even if it was not always recognized as such. It had the ability to defend itself, to see to it that its essential rights were respected, and gradually to take a place in the concert of Europe, which was just what happened. Despite some unhappy episodes, despite some mistakes in foreign policy, our judgment of the international position attained by Italy in the fifty years of unity must on the whole and in all conscience be positive. The post-Risorgimento generation did not betray the inheritance entrusted to it, even if it did not always administer it well.

At the time when the Risorgimento was coming to political and territorial fulfillment, the Piedmontese and then the Italian government had leaned chiefly on the French alliance. Even 1866 brought no substantial change, because the Prussian alliance was somehow made to fit in with the French; moreover, after the war the Prussian alliance was ended. Nevertheless, Mentana and the subsequent obstinacy of Napoleon III with regard to Rome loosened the French tie. Then the war of 1870 overturned the Napoleonic empire and radically changed the situation. A new opposition between the moderates and the Action Party came into existence. The moderates preferred the policy of the free hand, whereas the Action Party favored alliance with Germany. The royal visits in 1873 to Vienna and Berlin represented a compromise between the two tendencies. After the rapid, vague illusions of 1877 (alliance with Germany and Russia against Austria), and the disappointments of the Congress of Berlin, the roles were almost reversed, reflecting the change that had taken place in France: the major opposition to the alliance with the Central Powers came from the Left, and the major support came from the Right, though the Left was in power when the alliance was made. The royal will and royal considerations played the decisive role; dynastic-conservative interests were worried about the republicans being allied to France and at the same time Irredentist against Austria. Fifteen years of unadulterated Triple Alliance ended amidst the disasters of Crispi's second ministry. Then there was a slow return to the other direction, supported directly by those elements in the Right that wanted to take up the old tradition. There came the understanding with France, and then also with Russia, while the Triple Alliance was reduced to a mere element of European statics. Throughout these changes, friendship with England was an uncontested, fixed policy. It was based on mutual interest in maintaining a balance in the Mediterranean (against France, eventually also against Russia), and was traceable to the favorable attitude of English public opinion and of the English government itself toward the Italian revolution and unity (Russell's famous note of October 27, 1860, in favor of the self-determination of the people).

Substantially, Italian foreign policy in all its various phases (especially the last) was a policy of equilibrium. As the smallest and youngest among the great European powers, located at the edge of the Continent, Italy's primary concern was that no power become dominant or pre-eminent in Europe. It was a translation into practical political terms of the precious inheritance of the Risorgimento: national independence. This interest completely prevailed over any notion of expansion. It accounts for the caution toward Irredentism even after its republican, antidynastic character had been eliminated. And yet, all prudence notwithstanding, important gains were made in Tripoli, the Balkans, and the eastern Mediterranean.

The alliance with Austria was in contrast with the traditions and ideals of the Risorgimento. It was not just a question of renouncing Irredentism, which in any case would have had to be put aside because of the general European situation (even France could not have its war for Alsace-Lorraine): aside from Irredentism, there was the matter of policy toward the Balkan peoples and the Slavic and Rumanian nationalities in Austria-Hungary. The two orientations, moderate (Balbo) and Mazzinian, came into conflict once again. Article 7 of the Triple

Alliance represented something of a sop (compensation for Italy in case of Austro-Hungarian occupation in the Balkans); in reality, that article kept things on the level of the old politics. We were committed to the policy of preserving Austria-Hungary and Turkey, whose destinies, as Mazzini had intuited, were more linked than ever. If preservation had gone together with evolution and with preparation for the liberty and national organization of the peoples in the two empires, things would have been fine. But that was not the case, and for that Italy cannot be held responsible. The consequences were the war of 1914 and the Danubian-Balkan revolutions of 1918.

CHAPTER VII

The Post-Risorgimento Crisis

1. *Mussolini and Nationalism*

The outbreak of war in Europe at the beginning of August, 1914, shook the foundations of Italian foreign policy, which was based on an alliance with one of the two groups in the war, and on an understanding with the members of the other group. And the tremor almost immediately made itself felt in domestic affairs. A crisis began for the Italian state of the post-Risorgimento, a crisis that grew more intense in the years 1915–22, exploded in the following years, and turned into a catastrophe.

If someone had taken stock of the political development of Italy on the eve of the First World War—the fiftieth anniversary of the kingdom offered the best occasion for it—he would have found that it had reached its culminating point. Italy was realizing itself as a national, liberal, and social democracy (cf. above, pp. 178–9). There was nevertheless a general factor of weakness in the limited scope of political education, which kept the base of the ruling class restricted. Italian political life was like an adolescent with a delicate constitution: he appears full of youthful exuberance, but is not yet secure against diseases dangerous to his existence.

It is precisely to diseases of that sort that we can compare the two new factors that appeared on the Italian political scene on the eve of the war. Because of them, we must affirm that the Italian domestic crisis actually preceded the foreign crisis. The two new factors were Mussolini's Socialism and Nationalism, at that time apparently in extreme opposition, but in reality very much alike and destined to fuse within a few years.

The revival of revolution in Italian Socialism, during and immediately after the Libyan war, was something quite different from the intransigent tendency within the Socialist Party throughout the preceding decade—the tendency to fight reform. Benito Mussolini did not care one bit about collaboration with bourgeois parties and governments; instead, in opposition to the entire development of Socialism from Marx on, he advocated direct action as the normal method in political struggle. Mussolini rejected the normal rules of parties, parliamentary life, the liberal method, and progressive and consensual evolution. His spirit was akin to the earlier syndicalism, transposing the methods and spirit of the trade-union struggle to the political struggle. The general inspiration came from Georges Sorel, whose words were widely preached in Italy from the most diverse pulpits, and from whom many people learned the cult of violence and the hatred of democracy.

In that cult and in that hatred, Mussolini's neo-revolutionary ideas came in touch with Nationalism. This movement was born in Italy in the years immediately preceding the Libyan war, and grew during the war to national importance. The initiators came from the most diverse places: from the conservative-liberal camp, from Irredentist democracy, and from syndicalism. At first, they fraternized amidst a general patriotic enthusiasm for the elevation and greatness of Italy; but behind this general patriotism there was a political doctrine, an ideology, and a method of political struggle that assumed ever more precise features, while a parallel process of secession and regrouping was going on in the inner circle. The ideology of Italian Nationalism was a combination of Spencerian positivism (struggle for existence, natural selection, survival of the fittest) and of German statism, Hegelian or neo-Hegelian, fused in the doctrinal mold of the French nationalism of Daudet and Maurras. The fusion was impregnated with jingoist and imperialistic rhetoric, and with pugnacious, heroicizing, antihumanitarian Nietzscheanism. The master of both forms was Gabriele D'Annunzio. It was an ideology bearing many marks, almost all of them foreign, completely alien to the Italian traditions of the Risorgimento, and directly opposed to its liberal and humanitarian spirit. Italian Nationalism consciously rejected that spirit, declaring that the only important thing in the Risorgimento had been the formation of the territorial state. The ideals of the Risorgimento were to be considered simply instruments useful for that formation, to be thrown away after the completion as useless encumbrances— or, rather, to be eliminated because they were sources of dissolution. The ideal of Nationalism was the destruction of liberalism, democracy, and Socialism, in favor of the despotic dominance of the state, a purely abstract and formal entity on its theoretical outline, but one which in practice assumed the function of an idol: Moloch swallowing the citizens sacrificed to the god. It was a resurrection of the ancient absolute state, but much worse because its power and its will were extended without limits, and the old moral content was abandoned. And so Nationalism came forth as a more bitter and aggravated form of the anti-Risorgimento.

With this sort of ideology, Nationalism could only find support among the most retrograde elements of the nation. Such support came from the money of the steel industry and the votes of the clericals. They were enticed by the anti-Masonic and antiliberal struggle of Nationalism, by the large part it reserved for ecclesiastical influence, and by the exaltation of the papacy (politically, not religiously) as a basic constituent element of Italian greatness. The alliance with the most outspoken clericals completed and unveiled the clear anti-Risorgimento character of Nationalism. And yet, despite its blatantly antiliberal character, it penetrated the liberal camp broadly, inasmuch as Italian liberals had become simply anti-Socialist, conservative, and in fact reactionary. Soured by their exclusion from power, they thought only of getting it back by any means; the more extremist among them committed disruptive deeds that made them qualify as anarchists. These "liberal" sympathizers and "right-minded men" were impressed by the methods Nationalism had taken over from the "subversives": violent language and gestures, personal aggressiveness, and disturbances in the streets. In other words, the reactionary content was realized through demagogic methods: an alliance which, with the complicity of the "anarchical conservatives," was to become a key to Italian politics in the postwar period.

2. *From the May Days to the March on Rome*

The foreign policy of the Nationalists was imperialistic, directed solely toward the physical expansion of the nation, without regard for the ideal principles and the universal values of international order. Here, too, in other words, it was in direct opposition to the Risorgimento—be it the Risorgimento of Cavour or, even more, of Mazzini. They supported the German alliance; in fact, they considered it permanent and necessary, because they were hoping for a war of conquest in the Mediterranean and in the colonies, with France and England the losers. Nor did they care anything about the fundamental problem of reordering Europe in a satisfactory way. The declaration of Italian neutrality and the general disposition of the Italians induced them to reverse themselves and, without many scruples, to go over to the anti-German camp and try to lead it.

With the Austrian attack on Serbia and the European war that followed, the thirty-year-old Italian policy of the Triple Alliance was shaken to its foundations. By now, the preoccupation with defense against France had disappeared, whereas the preoccupation with Austrian expansion in the Balkans had grown enormously. The conservative-dynastic motive for the Triple Alliance, originally so important, had now lost all efficacy because of domestic Italian developments. On the other hand, Irredentism, no longer tied to antidynastic republicanism, was making a triumphant return; and with it returned the tradition of the Risorgimento and the national-democratic ideology (of which the Triple Entente was champion), with strong support from Francophile Masonry, which was widespread throughout Italy.

The Italian Nationalists seemed to adhere to this ideology, abandoning their imperialistic and reactionary conceptions. In reality, though, they brought their spirit and especially their demagogy intact into the democratic camp. The same can be said of Mussolini's move from the neutrality of the Socialist Party to interventionism, a move that enabled him to stand together with the revolutionary syndicalists. In all three cases, the *spiritus rector*, the guiding motive, was that of war for the sake of war, violence used to demolish the old liberal-democratic-pacifist world. This spirit was in direct contrast to the spirit that reigned in the democratic wing of interventionism. The democratic wing was numerically and even politically far superior to the other, if we look at the positions its members held; but in the struggle for intervention and in the subsequent conflicts with neutralism, it was largely dominated by the demagogic "dynamism" of its allies-enemies. The neutralist front was not much more homogeneous than the interventionist amalgam: conservatives who might be defined neutralists of fear; Catholics, largely inspired by confessional motives; Socialists, dogmatically pacifistic and obedient to mechanical party discipline; and, finally, pure nationalists, "nonparty men" who wanted an undifferentiated neutrality, ready to take advantage of any occasion for the protection and aggrandizement of Italy, unaware of the universal, ideological, and passionate forces that had been unleashed by the European conflict. The whole array of Italian politics and the very structure of the parties was shaken by the new division between interventionists and neutralists, while the further political development of the post-Risorgimento—i.e., the formation of a national democracy—was arrested and compromised.

The May days brought the turmoil to an extreme. With the clamorous, crushing victory of the interventionists over the neutralists (annihilating whatever use neutralism may have had from the point of view of national policy), there was the victory of the "piazza" over parliament; and Giolitti, the head of the parliamentary majority, was defamed as a traitor and banished from national life. It meant the collapse of the entire political-parliamentary situation that had formed after 1900, a situation that had supported the political-social development of the country, joining liberal democracy and Socialism in the "popular blocs" and in parliament. With its passive opposition in principle to the war, Socialism withdrew to the margin of national life; and the conservative-reactionary forces, which would have liked to eject it entirely, got the upper hand. The democratic interventionist majority rejected its former leader and allies and accepted their national excommunication, while the neutralist minority for the most part limited itself to a sour policy of recriminatory pinpricking. What dominated the situation was a mixture of Nationalism and Fascism, which was just born. And so the war that was called—and, in a certain sense, was—the last war of the Risorgimento opened with a profound moral scission, into which the anti-Risorgimento thrust its poisoned steel. The monarchy could have and should have intervened, by pronouncing words of peace and reconciliation for the defense and salvation of someone who had after all been its own man. But either because of moral incomprehension or Machiavellian design, the monarchy deserted its task. It was only the first of its desertions in the thirty-year period that saw the fatal transition from the post-Risorgimento to the anti-Risorgimento.

The scission and the quarrel between interventionists and neutralists meandered throughout the entire war. The current of patriotism, which flowed broadly and impetuously especially after Caporetto, was not enough to eliminate those differences; and the disputes on the causes of that defeat and later on the results of the war only served to revive them. Nevertheless, for a while after the war there was a reconciliation between interventionist democracy and neutralist democracy; but they could neither re-establish a majority in parliament nor bring about a political situation of liberal and social democracy in the country. There was a miserable flaking off of parliamentary groups, with new and old personal antagonisms coming to the fore. With liberals and democrats pulverized, the new forces of Maximalist Socialism, Popularism, and Fascism contested the field.

The first two emerged triumphant from the elections of 1919, marking the removal from authority of the old ruling class without substituting a new one. Maximalist Socialism, which was revolutionary in word but certainly not in deed, perpetuated the division, formed by the war, between the proletariat and democracy. The horizons of the Populars, who had attracted a good number of the liberal-conservative troops, did not go beyond particularistic and confessional politics. Exploiting the most varied sentiments and interests, Fascism drew its recruits from the jumbled multitude that had no political consciousness and no class consistency, the men without party. It took advantage of the malcontent of the petty-bourgeois "veterans," of apocalyptic patriotism (also predominantly petty-bourgeois) exacerbated by an occasional (and cleverly exaggerated) excess on the part of posthumous Socialist neutralism. It was exacerbated even more by the myth of the "mutilated" or "betrayed" victory, a Machiavellian-demagogic creation of Nationalism. (In reality, from a purely political-territorial point of view, no nation gained as much from the war as Italy. The real damage, not only to Italy but to all of Europe, had to be looked for elsewhere.) Above all, Fascism took advantage of the fear of Bolshevism. It was backed vigorously by landowners, industrialists, Masons, "liberals," and above all by Nationalists, who became ever more the true inspirers of the movement. Very soon, it lost the few national-democratic features it had originally possessed, and assumed a frankly reactionary, anti-Risorgimento physiognomy.

Fascism, with Mussolini as Duce, drew its method of direct action (that is, of physical violence) from Nationalism, Syndicalism, and above all from the commando mentality of the war, and used it against Socialism, and then against all adversaries. The political activity of Fascism flourished by applying these methods, while the state authorities and the leading classes were either inert or accomplices. Then came the "March on Rome," which would have failed (and with that Fascism would have been liquidated) if the king had not shattered the weapon of defense which the legal government had in hand, and called to power the leader of the revolt against the constitution and against the national state of the Risorgimento.

3. From the March on Rome to Totalitarian Fascism

With that call, King Victor Emmanuel III of Savoy-Carignano made himself directly and primarily responsible for all the anti-constitutional, antiliberal, and anti-Risorgimento deeds of the Fascist regime. At first, his attitude was somewhat ambiguous, thanks to Mussolini's ability to balance pure Fascism and "liberal" philo-Fascism. A typical manifestation of that ambiguity was the government's "big list" for the elections in 1924. After the Matteotti murder and the anti-Fascist reactions (which were immobilized by the passivity of the "Aventine"), all ambiguity disappeared; even most "liberals" were now forced into a belated and impotent opposition. Having routed all opposition with the force of the state and the party, Mussolini completed the construction of his Fascist dictatorial-totalitarian state; and National-Fascism (Nationalists and Fascists had fused even formally soon after the

"March on Rome") realized itself fully as anti-Risorgimento. It brought the suppression of all liberties, the discrediting and destruction of parliament, justice subservient to political power, party privilege annulling equality among citizens, exploitation of the national economy for the advantage of bands of profiteers, and the subjection and pollution of national culture through gross and inconsistent conceptions hostile to the humanistic principles fundamental to the new Italy.

A necessary accomplice in this work of destruction was the crown, which gave a free hand to Fascism, and contributed to the spontaneous manifestations of adherence to Fascism. By doing that, King Victor Emmanuel III failed to live up to the oath he took and the commitments he made upon ascending the throne; he reversed the policy he had followed before the war, abandoned the legal foundations and the moral traditions with which the Italian monarchy had emerged from the Risorgimento, and destroyed the very substance of the monarchy, which consisted precisely in the association of the Savoyard dynasty with the liberty and self-government of the nation. Between 1922 and 1926, the monarchy that had existed in Italy since 1861 faded away, and was replaced by an indefinite and indefinable institution, devoid both of legal basis and political-moral consistency. It was not a return to the ancient absolutism of the Savoyard monarchs of the first branch (which would not have been legitimate or justified, in any case). As a matter of fact, the Fascist regime as a political actuality, and with its uncertain and crude attempts to formulate ideology, was the very negation of such a monarchy. By attributing to the king and to the king alone the right to select and discharge the head of government, and the right to sanction all governmental acts, Fascism was producing a hybrid of party totalitariansim and Ducist dictatorship combined with the royal will, and doing it in such a way that the final responsibility for everything fell upon the king. In practice, although the king was reduced to the function of putting his seal on acts of the regime, he was covering those acts with the authority and the prestige of the monarchy. That was important above all for the army, whose leaders had never got over the feudal-absolutistic concept of personal loyalty to the king, and who therefore found in the sanction given by the king to the regime the justification to tolerate or promote the Fascistization of the national army, the results of which were seen in September, 1943.

After the monarchy, the upper bourgeoisie (and especially the so-called plutocrats) supported and abetted the regime. They renounced what after all had been the *raison d'être* of capitalistic enterprise (economic initiative responsible for increase in production), and accepted instead all the caprices and failures of the Fascist economy. In exchange, they got personal profit, acquired in a closed and dictatorially regulated economy. They also got the destruction of proletarian syndicalism, and of the moral personality of the worker. We might add to this list of accomplices of Fascism the conservatives, men blind with sectarianism and fear, and deniers of every authentic principle of conservatism. We might also add that a large portion of the intelligentsia practiced an opportunistic conformism toward the regime, sowing confusion in men's minds and perversion in their hearts.

The understanding with the Vatican reinforced the subjugation of the Italian people. It was founded—or, at least, manifested itself—in the Lateran agreements (1929). We must distinguish clearly the material content of these agreements from the political-moral conditions under which they were drawn up, and from the results they produced for the general Italian situation. The settlement of the Roman Question (Vatican City) was based on solutions envisaged in the Risorgimento and in the post-Risorgimento, and was little more than a bilateral recasting of the Law of Guarantees. We could give a more varied and complex judgment of the Concordat, based on the different clauses and certain statements of principle; but this is not the place to do it. The main point to be considered in this historical foreshortening of ours is the political moment in which these agreements were drawn up, their *Sitz im Leben*, to use a very effective German expression—in other words, the place they found and the vital function they performed within the total crisis of Italian political life.

The beginning of the negotiations coincided with the time of the full installation of Mussolini's Fascist dictatorship, erected on the ruins of the old liberal-democratic regime, the only legal regime, the only one that could claim to represent the free will of the Italian people. The agreements were concluded on the body of a servile, afflicted Italy; they coincided with the expulsion from parliament of legitimate representatives of the people, the final suppression of all liberties, and with political exile and the Special Tribunal. The inevitable moral effect was that the pope and the Church endorsed what Fascism had done, and endorsed the man whom the pontiff, on the day after the agreement, called a providential man. This effect was confirmed by the official intervention of the Catholics in favor of the regime in the "elections" that followed immediately. A natural result was the understanding that established itself throughout Italy between the ecclesiastical hierarchy and Fascism, an understanding which not only riveted the shackles of the Italian people but also gave the final and most effective touches to the anti-Risorgimento character of the new regime, in the form of "clerico-Fascism." Neither the violent but brief conflict between the Fascist government and the Holy See over Catholic Action (1931) nor the occasional contrasts between the two powers did anything to change this state of affairs. Only in the last days of the pontificate of Pius XI was there any sense of distance between Palazzo Venezia and the Vatican.

4. *The Catastrophe*

In foreign policy, the liberal regime had left the Fascist regime a precious inheritance: the Treaty of Rapallo. It was precious because of the specific provisions of the treaty, and because of the possibilities and the promise it contained. Rapallo, together with the earlier Treaty of Saint-Germain, had completed the work of the Risorgimento; it assured Italy a territorial settlement so favorable that any attempt on our part to question it had to be considered antinational. At the same time, it established a basis for collaboration between Italy and the young Balkan nationalities, a direction that had already been indicated by the genius of Mazzini as the main road for the security and greatness of our nation.

Fascism accepted the inheritance of Rapallo materially, but without appropriating its spirit, which it found unintelligible. This lack of intelligence had a counterpart in Yugoslav and particularly in Croatian nationalism. Relations with Yugoslavia were getting worse all the time. The gradual strengthening of ties among the Balkan nations (including Turkey) took place not because of Italian influence but in opposition to it. The only field of activity open to Italian influence was Bulgarian Irredentism, and that was the exact opposite of the pacificatory role it should have played. With the Little Entente, the good relations begun at the time of Rapallo gave way to a spirit of hostility and to exclusive French influence. With regard to Germany and the German problem, Mussolini began his government by putting himself behind Poincaré's unintelligent policy; he therefore maintained a passive attitude toward the policy of Locarno, kept himself aloof from the republican Germany of Stresemann, and showed himself hostile, or at least contemptuous, toward the League of Nations and the ideals of European pacification and collaboration. After 1930, Fascism began demagogically waving the banner of revisionism, just at the time when the evacuation of the Rhine and the new settlement, or liquidation, of reparations had healed the worst wounds of Versailles, and when the ascent of German National Socialism—favored by Fascism—threatened the peace of Europe and the state of affairs that guaranteed the fruits of Italian victory.

When Hitler revealed his appetite for Austria, Mussolini had a lucid moment, evidenced in his "Stresa policy"; that is, the understanding with the Western Powers. But the irremediable myopia of National-Fascism led it to conceive of and practice that policy on the basis of the small-minded and opportunistic *do ut des*. Then this matter of basic, vital Italian interest was deferred in favor of the craving for colonial conquest and the grotesque dream of a "resurrection of the empire," which led to the Ethiopian adventure. From that adventure resulted the remilitarization of the Rhine, prelude to the second European war. Mussolini lent a strong hand to the achievements of Hitlerian imperialism with the policy of the "Rome-Berlin Axis," which was inspired by interests of the Fascist Party. That brought the offensive and defensive alliance of the Pact of Steel, which put Italy at the mercy of Hitler; and it brought participation in the war unleashed by Hitler for the National Socialist domination of Europe and the world, and for the destruction of Latin, European, and Christian civilization. Italy was thus forced into a war in which defeat would have meant losing a great deal, and victory would have meant losing everything: independence, liberty, honor, and even its reason for being. It was the final apostasy of the Risorgimento, the supreme betrayal of the nation. Once again, the Savoyard monarchy was the necessary accomplice in the apostasy and betrayal, thus sealing its own fate, which had already been determined fifteen years earlier. Through the Savoyard monarchy, the post-Risorgimento had ended in the anti-Risorgimento. Italian institutional development, suspended by the plebiscites, now ceased altogether; the compromise brought about by the constitutional monarchy faded away. The Italian people, left on their own by the dynastic betrayal, had no choice but to take their destiny into their own hands.

Index